GCSE 9-1

geography

AQA

T0347611

SECOND EDITION

Exam Practice

Grades 4-6

SERIES EDITORS

Bob Digby

Simon Ross   **Nicholas Rowles**

OXFORD

OXFORD
UNIVERSITY PRESS

Great Clarendon Street, Oxford, OX2 6DP, United Kingdom

Oxford University Press is a department of the University of Oxford. It furthers the University's objective of excellence in research, scholarship, and education by publishing worldwide. Oxford is a registered trade mark of Oxford University Press in the UK and in certain other countries

© Oxford University Press 2023

Series Editors: Bob Digby, Simon Ross

Author: Nicholas Rowles

The moral rights of the authors have been asserted

First published in 2020

Second edition 2023

British Library Cataloguing in Publication Data
Data available

ISBN 978-138-202905-6

Ebook ISBN 978-138-202906-3

10 9 8 7 6 5 4 3 2

Paper used in the production of this book is a natural, recyclable product made from wood grown in sustainable forests.

The manufacturing process conforms to the environmental regulations of the country of origin.

Printed in India by Manipal Technologies Limited

Acknowledgements
The publisher and authors would like to thank the following for permission to use photographs and other copyright material:

Cover: watchara/Shutterstock; Billion Photos/Shutterstock. **Photos: p9:** Washington Imaging / Alamy Stock Photo; **p11:** Jason Knott / Alamy Stock Photo; **p14 (l):** Jemastock/Shutterstock; **p14 (m):** Quarta/Shutterstock; **p14 (r):** Man As Thep/Shutterstock; **p14:** Geoffrey Robinson / Alamy Stock Photo; **p17 (t):** BlueRingMedia/Shutterstock; **p17 (b):** ZUMA Press, Inc. / Alamy Stock Photo; **p18:** Designervn/Shutterstock; **p19:** Blaine Harrington III / Alamy Stock Photo; **p21:** robertharding / Alamy Stock Photo; **p27:** Kevin Foy / Alamy Stock Photo; **p31:** kylauf/Shutterstock; **p33:** geogphotos / Alamy Stock Photo; **p38:** Ann Rayworth / Alamy Stock Photo; **p39:** © Crown copyright 2020 OS100000249; **p45:** Harvepino/Shutterstock; **p49:** © Bob Digby; **p56:** RomeoFox / Alamy Stock Photo; **p57:** domnitsky/Shutterstock; **p58:** RomeoFox / Alamy Stock Photo; **p61:** domnitsky/Shutterstock; **p69:** Stuart Kelly / Alamy Stock Photo; **p70:** © NASA; **p72:** cgwp.co.uk / Alamy Stock Photo; **p73:** domnitsky/Shutterstock; **p74:** cgwp.co.uk / Alamy Stock Photo; **p76:** Minden Pictures / Alamy Stock Photo; **p77:** domnitsky/Shutterstock; **p79:** Minden Pictures / Alamy Stock Photo; **p82:** domnitsky/Shutterstock; **p87:** domnitsky/Shutterstock; **p94:** Anya Douglas/Shutterstock; **p100:** Kevin Eaves/Shutterstock; **p105 (t):** Anya Douglas/Shutterstock; **p105 (b):** NOAA / Alamy Stock Photo; **p108:** Kekyalyaynen/Shutterstock; **p118:** © Nick Rowles; **p120 (t,l):** Valerijs Novickis/Shutterstock; **p120 (t,r):** Dirk Ercken/Shutterstock; **p120 (b,l):** buddhawut/Shutterstock; **p120 (b,r):** soubeoi/Shutterstock; **p124:** Dorset Media Service / Alamy Stock Photo; **p127:** wonganan/Getty Images; **p130:** Dave Ellison / Alamy Stock Photo; **p139 (l):** zvimages/Getty Images; **p139 (r):** alexsl/Getty Images; **p157:** robertharding / Alamy Stock Photo; **p158:** Jo-Anne Albertsen / Alamy Stock Photo; **p164:** agefotostock / Alamy Stock Photo; **p165 (a):** sydeen/

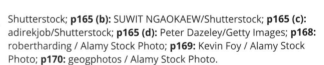

Shutterstock; **p165 (b):** SUWIT NGAOKAEW/Shutterstock; **p165 (c):** adirekjob/Shutterstock; **p165 (d):** Peter Dazeley/Getty Images; **p168:** robertharding / Alamy Stock Photo; **p169:** Kevin Foy / Alamy Stock Photo; **p170:** geogphotos / Alamy Stock Photo.

Artwork by Barking Dog Art, Kamae, Q2A Media, Aptara Inc, Mike Phillips and Oxford University Press.

Every effort has been made to contact copyright holders of material reproduced in this book. Any omissions will be rectified in subsequent printings if notice is given to the publisher.

Links to third party websites are provided by Oxford in good faith and for information only. Oxford disclaims any responsibility for the materials contained in any third party website referenced in this work.

The publisher would like to thank Katy Patchwood for reviewing this book and providing thoughtful and constructive feedback.

Contents

Guided answers and mark schemes for the exam practice papers are available on the Oxford Secondary Geography website: **www.oxfordsecondary.com/geog-aqa-answers**

Please note: the exam-style questions and mark schemes have not been written or approved by AQA. The answer guidance and commentaries provided represent one interpretation only and other solutions may be appropriate.

Introduction

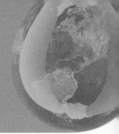

About this book

What are the aims of *Exam Practice: Grades 4–6*?

GCSE 9-1 Geography AQA Exam Practice: Grades 4–6 is a practical workbook for you to complete. It is full of useful advice and practice that will help you to achieve or better your target grade.

The book can be used to support your learning at any point in your course, including when revising for exams. There are plenty of activities and exam-style questions to help you practise and develop the skills needed for exam success.

How is the book organised?

There are five main sections:

> **1 Top tips for exam success** (pages 6–13)
>
> This focuses on key aspects of exam technique, such as interpreting command words, maximising resources such as photos and graphs, and understanding how your answers are marked.
>
> **2 Getting to grips with...** (pages 14–23)
> **Upgrade your topic knowledge** (pages 24–35)
>
> The AQA specification includes concepts that can be tricky to fully understand, such as development, sustainability and scale, as well as key topics such as ecosystems, natural hazards and resource management. Mastering these concepts and topics helps to improve the quality of your answers.
>
> **3 On your marks** (pages 36–91)
>
> This section shows you how to maximise your marks for each type of question, including multiple-choice, short-answer and extended-writing questions. Here you will have many opportunities to attempt practice questions. You will also see how an examiner will mark your answer.
>
> **4 Focus on Paper 3: Geographical applications** (pages 92–108)
>
> This section focuses on the two parts of Paper 3 – issue evaluation (Section A) and fieldwork (Section B). It includes a resources booklet for you to practise with.
>
> **5 Exam practice papers** (pages 113–166)
>
> This final section provides you with a complete set of exam papers for you to practise all that you have learned.

> In these sections, quick **Activities** test your knowledge, while **Worked examples** break down how to approach exam questions. You can apply what you've learned to answer exam-style questions in **Now try this!**

> **Answer guidance** for all the Activities and 'Now try this!' questions can be found in the back of this book. **Mark schemes** for the exam papers can be found at **www.oxfordsecondary. com/geog-aqa-answers**.

How to be successful in your exams

It's not what you know...

... but what you do with it! Your success depends on your ability to adapt your extensive geographical knowledge to the demands of the exam questions. You will need to:

- identify what the question is asking you to do
- answer it precisely and concisely
- demonstrate your geographical knowledge (including your examples and case studies)
- interpret resources, such as photos and graphs, that you have never seen before.

Some student traits... do you recognise yourself?

To improve, you first have to recognise your weaknesses. For example, **admitting to yourself** that you have a fear of flying is the first step towards solving the problem and getting on a plane.

 **Activity 1**

Read the descriptions around the cartoon below.

(a) Be honest, and highlight any characteristics that you recognise in yourself.

(b) Can you think of **two** more characteristics that apply to you? Complete the blank boxes.

(c) In the Action Plan below, identify **three** key aspects to address to maximise your full potential.

I often run out of time and have to leave some questions unanswered.

I am a bit lazy and don't revise enough.

I tend to rush and make silly mistakes.

I tend to write too much and my teacher says I waffle!

I am not very precise when using resources such as photos and graphs.

There are some Geography topics or geographical terms that I don't fully understand.

I have difficulty interpreting some questions.

My answers sometimes lack depth and detail.

Action Plan

To maximise my potential, I need to focus on making the following improvements:

- _____

- _____

- _____

Organisation is the key to success

Students who do well in exams are usually well organised. They know the specification, they have correctly sequenced and detailed notes, and they know the requirements of each exam.

Here's what you can do:

- Make sure your notes are clearly structured to reflect the exam papers and topics. ☐

- Consider highlighting key geographical terms in your notes and revising their definitions. Good use of geographical vocabulary will help boost your mark and contribute towards SPaG (Spelling, Punctuation and Grammar) marks. ☐

- Make sure you know where the examples, case studies and geographical skills are within your notes. ☐

- Plan your revision well in advance, working backwards from the date of your exams. ☐

- Complete the specification and skills confidence checklists on pages 109–112 of this book as you go. ☐

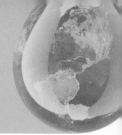

Top tips for exam success

1. Understand the specification

Look at the specification outline below. There are three exam papers with roughly the same number of marks available for each. Organise your notes carefully to reflect the structure and content of the specification. (A more detailed version of the specification is available on pages 109–110 and on the AQA website.)

Paper 1	Paper 2	Paper 3
Living with the physical environment: 88 marks (35%), 1 hr 30 min	Challenges in the human environment: 88 marks (35%), 1 hr 30 min	Geographical applications: 76 marks (30%), 1 hr 15 min
Date:	**Date:**	**Date:**
Challenge of natural hazards: tectonic hazards, tropical storms, extreme weather in the UK, climate change	**Urban challenges:** global patterns, two contrasting cities, sustainable urban futures	**Issue evaluation:** critical thinking and problem solving based on pre-release resources booklet, including a decision-making exercise
The living world: local ecosystems, tropical rainforests, **one** from *hot deserts, cold environments*	**The changing economic world:** global patterns, closing the development gap, contrasting studies of economic development (*UK and one city in LIC/NEE*)	**Fieldwork:** general questions based on enquiry process together with questions on the two (physical and human) individual student investigations
Physical landscapes in the UK: two from *coastal, river, glacial landscapes*	**Challenge of resource management:** global resource security, resources in the UK, **one** from *food, water, energy*	

Activity 2

(a) In this table, write the date and time that you will be sitting each exam.

(b) Use a highlighter to identify the optional topics that you are taking.

2. Understand command words

A 'command' is an order to do something. In an exam question, the 'command word' directs your focus when answering a question (e.g. it tells you whether to 'describe' or 'explain' something). You need to understand the command words and make sure you stick to them rigidly.

Command word	Typical marks	Meaning	Student advice
Identify/state/ give	1	Name, find or give a simple word or statement. E.g. 'Identify the glacial landform at grid reference 653532.'	Usually a simple and direct question requiring a precise and accurate answer.
Calculate	1 or 2	Work out the value of something. E.g. 'Using Figure 7, calculate the increase in the retail sales value of Fairtrade bananas between 2000 and 2012.'	Be precise. Double-check your calculation. Give the correct units, e.g. kilometres or metres.
Complete	1 or 2	Finish the task by adding information. E.g. 'Complete the following sentences.'	Should be simple – just double-check you have understood the question.
Compare	2, 3 or 4	Identify similarities and differences. E.g. 'Using Figure 4, compare HDI values in Africa and South America.'	Look for both similarities and differences. Use words like 'whereas' or 'as opposed to' when talking about differences.

Outline	2 or 4	Set out main characteristics and give an overview. E.g. 'Outline one way that Fairtrade helps to deal with the problems of unequal development.'	A relatively brief overview of the key points or characteristics.
Describe	2 or 4	Set out more detailed characteristics. E.g. 'Using Figure 9, describe the distribution of areas with existing licences for fracking in the UK.'	Write what you can see. This might include shape, size and colour. With data, include highest and lowest values, rate of increase or decrease.
Explain	2, 4, 6 or 9	Give reasons why something happens. E.g. 'Using Figure 12 and your own knowledge, explain how different landforms may be created by the transport and deposition of sediment along the coast.'	Give reasons why something has formed or occurred. This requires you to show your understanding. Use the word 'because'.
Suggest	2, 4, 6 or 9	Give a possible reason. E.g. 'Suggest how the sea defences shown in Figure 11 help to protect the coastline.'	Put forward an idea/outcome/judgement/point of view. Usually requires evidence in support.
To what extent	6 or 9	Judge the importance or success of a strategy/scheme/project. E.g. 'To what extent do urban areas in lower income countries (LICs) or newly emerging economies (NEEs) provide social and economic opportunities for people?'	Imagine a line that extends from 0–100%, or yes–no or good–bad. Where is your opinion on that imaginary line and why? Words like 'mostly' or 'strongly' might work well.
Assess (may be 'Assess the extent to which...')	6 or 9	Make an informed judgement by weighing up most/least important factors. E.g. 'Assess how effective your presentation technique(s) were in representing the data collected in this enquiry.'	Use evidence to judge the level of success or importance, for example. Use words like 'very', 'not very', 'extremely well', 'poorly', etc.
Evaluate	9	Judge from available evidence, often giving both sides of an argument or referring to +/- points. E.g. 'Evaluate the effectiveness of an urban transport scheme(s) you have studied.'	Use evidence to weigh up and make judgements. Often to do with levels of success or effectiveness. Make comparisons and use words like 'whereas' or 'on the other hand'.
Discuss	6 or 9	Present key points about different ideas or strengths and weaknesses of an idea. E.g. 'Discuss the effects of urban sprawl on people and the environment.'	Give both sides of an argument – pros and cons, advantages and disadvantages. Try to be balanced. Words like 'whereas' are good.
Justify	9	Support a case or decision using evidence. E.g. 'Transnational corporations (TNCs) only bring advantages to the host country. Do you agree with this statement? Justify your decision.'	Back up your views or a decision. Refer to evidence to support your answer.

Activity 3

Draw lines to match up the command words with their correct meanings.

State	Judge the importance of, for example, an outcome or decision
Calculate	Work out something (usually statistical)
Suggest	Provide a simple statement (often a fact)
To what extent	Write what you can see
Explain	Use evidence to identify possible ideas or outcomes
Describe	Give reasons/say why something happens

Tip
The most commonly used command words tend to be 'give', 'state', 'outline', 'suggest', 'explain' and 'to what extent'.

3. Understand the question types

The exam papers are made up of several different types of question. These are outlined in the table below. (The 'On your marks' section of this book will help you to maximise your marks from different types of question.)

Question type	Common command words	Example	Student advice
Multiple choice (1 mark): involves making a choice of one from four options.	State, what, calculate	Calculate the area of the reservoir on the OS map extract. Is it…? (1 mark)	Multiple choice does not mean 'easy', so take time making your decision. Cross out the wrong answers to leave you with the correct answer.
Short-answer questions (1–3 marks): may involve factual recall or using a resource.	State, give, calculate (and show your working), outline, describe, suggest	Outline the role of decomposers in an ecosystem. (2 marks)	Try to be precise and don't waffle! Use correct geographical terminology. Refer to facts and figures (including measurement units).
Resource-focused questions (4/6 marks): often require detailed use of a resource together with your own understanding.	Describe, suggest, explain	Using Figure X and your own understanding, explain the effects of deindustrialisation on the UK's economy. (6 marks)	There are often several parts to these questions. In the example, you need to refer to Figure X, demonstrate your own understanding (refer to an example or outline a process), and make clear links between deindustrialisation and the UK's economy.
Extended-writing questions (6/9 marks): usually require engaging in a discussion or evaluation.	Assess, to what extent, discuss, justify	Using a case study of an LIC/NEE, evaluate the role of transnational corporations (TNCs) in promoting industrial development. (9 marks)	Have a go – do not leave it blank! Focus on the geography. Try to write about opposing views using your case study knowledge to support your arguments. Write a conclusion.

Deconstructing questions

Before starting to write an answer, take time to **deconstruct** the question. This will help you to identify what you need to write about.

To deconstruct a question, consider using '**BUG**':

- **B**ox the command word.

- **U**nderline words to pick out the geography content and focus, any evidence required (e.g. a resource or case study), and any links or connections required. Consider using colours, circling key words, or linking the connections required.

- **G**lance back to the question to make sure you include everything in your answer.

The 'On your marks' section in this book has many **BUG** examples and activities.

Worked example

'Use an example to ⬚explain⬚ how ⬭urban regeneration⬭ can help to

⬭solve urban problems⬭.' **[4 marks]**

🔍 Tip If there are words in a question that you do not understand, don't panic! Cross out those you don't understand and have a go at what is left. This will still pick you up some marks. Here's an example:

'Explain how river flooding can have ~~social and economic~~ impacts on communities.' **[4 marks]**

- If you're not sure of the meaning of 'social' and 'economic', cross them out.

- 'Impacts' is much easier, and some of the ones you write about are likely to be social and economic.

4. Understand the marking

There are two types of marking: '**point marking**' and '**levels marking**'. It is important that you recognise how each question will be marked.

- With point marked questions, you earn a mark for every correct point you make.

- With levels marked questions, you need to try to reach Level 2, or even Level 3, by showing your knowledge and understanding of the topic in the question, and making judgements.

> **Tip** The most important thing is to have a go at every question! Focus on the geography and you will pick up some marks.

	Point marking	Levels marking
Marks	1–3-mark questions	4-, 6- and 9-mark questions
Advice	Examiners are looking for precise, accurate points. For 2- and 3-mark questions, try to develop your answer to achieve maximum marks.	Examiners decide if answers belong to Level 1, 2 or 3: • **Level 1:** basic answer; limited application/knowledge or use of stimulus material • **Level 2:** clear understanding/application; good use of stimulus material; accurate use of locational information • **Level 3:** thorough/detailed knowledge, understanding and application; coherent argument; extensive use of examples/case studies

Activity 4

Read the exam question and sample answer below, then answer the questions that follow.

> Study **Figure 1**, a photo of High Force waterfall in County Durham. Using **Figure 1** and your own understanding, explain the processes involved in the formation of the waterfall. **[4 marks]**

Figure 1

Waterfalls are formed by the falling water which will erode the river bed and start to make a plunge pool. Rocks and other debris will be thrown around by the water and further erode out the plunge pool. The plunge pool will continue to grow and it will form an undercut below the cliff that the water is falling from. Eventually, it will collapse.

Read through the answer and complete the grid below.

Does the student...	Tick/cross and explanation
Make use of and refer to the photo?	
Write about more than one process?	✗ The term 'erode' is used but no specific terms (such as 'abrasion') are used
Write about the waterfall?	✔ The student does focus on the waterfall
Make links between processes and landforms?	✔ The student does link erosion to the formation of the plunge pool and undercutting of the 'cliff' (waterfall)
Show an understanding of the sequence of landform formation?	

> **Tip** It is very important to address **all** aspects of the question, particularly when you are required to use a figure, example or a case study. Consider using the sentence starter 'Figure 2 shows…'.

5. Make full use of the resources

Many exam questions use a resource, such as a photo, map, graph, table of data or extract of text. These questions usually begin 'Using Figure…'. When answering these questions you **must** use the resource to support your answer. This will help you to achieve a high-level mark.

Interpreting maps

Maps used in the exams include Ordnance Survey (OS) maps, maps showing global patterns (e.g. urbanisation) and maps showing locational details (e.g. the location of a science park).

Activity 5

Study **Figure 2**, a map of the global distribution of volcanoes. Using **Figure 2** and your own knowledge, describe the global distribution of volcanoes. **[4 marks]**

Figure 2

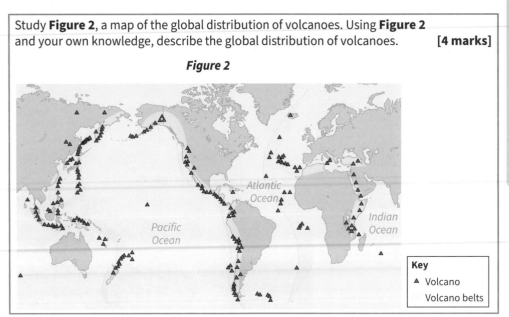

Key
▲ Volcano
Volcano belts

Figure 2 shows that volcanoes are widely distributed across the world. The map shows that most volcanoes form belts, for example around the edge of the Pacific Ocean (the so-called 'Ring of Fire'). Here, there is a line of volcanoes stretching through Japan, the Philippines and along the west coast of North and South America. Elsewhere, there are concentrations of volcanoes in East Africa, central Europe and in Iceland. While most volcanoes occur in these linear belts, there are some anomalies with isolated volcanoes in parts of Asia and Africa.

This is a top-quality answer. Underline or draw a circle to show where the student:

(a) refers to Figure 2
(b) refers to named parts of the world
(c) refers to an anomaly (exception).

Interpreting graphs

There are many different types of graph, including bar graphs, scattergraphs, pie charts and line graphs. You may be asked to complete a graph by plotting a value and shading an area. Every year, many students throw away easy marks by failing to complete graphs!

Tip Make full use of information in the key (the key is the key to success!). It will help you to answer the question. Most maps should have a scale and a north arrow. Use them when answering a question.

Tip When describing patterns on a map or a graph, consider using 'GCSE':
- **GC** – **g**eneral **c**omment (describe the overall pattern)
- **S** – **s**pecific (refer to names of places, locations or data)
- **E** – **e**xceptions (are there any anomalies to the general trend?)

Tip **Distribution** refers to 'where things are'. The word **pattern** can be used to describe a regular distribution; for example, 'it has a circular pattern'.

Activity 6

Study **Figure 3**, a graph of tourist arrivals in Nepal in 2019. Using **Figure 3**, describe the pattern of tourism in Nepal. **[4 marks]**

Use the following steps to annotate **Figure 3** to help you plan an answer.

(a) A circle has been drawn to identify the peak in March. Do the same for the peak in October and the trough in July.

(b) Use a ruler to draw vertical and horizontal lines to enable you to read accurate values for the peaks and trough. (The peak in March has already been done for you.)

(c) Locate the anomaly where, having risen from July, there is a slight dip in September.

(d) Use **Figure 3** to complete the gaps in the following answer.

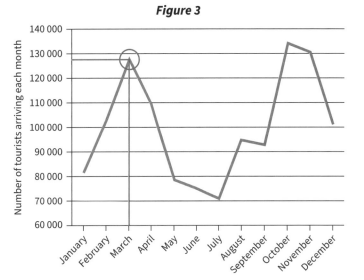
Figure 3

Figure 3 shows that tourist arrivals in Nepal fluctuated considerably during the year. The graph shows that tourist arrivals peaked in the months of _____ and October reaching about _____ tourists. The lowest number of arrivals was in July (about _____ tourists). In October, almost twice as many tourists arrived than in July. There is a general trend showing a decrease between March and July and an increase from July to October. However, there is a slight dip in _____. This is an anomaly.

> **Tip** Rather than simply quoting values from the graph, try to **manipulate** the data so you can make comparisons. For example, 'In October, almost twice as many tourists arrived than in July.'

Interpreting photos

Photos are often used in the exams. However, examiners often report that they are poorly used by students! You need to:

- look very closely at the details in a photo. Use locational language such as 'foreground', 'background', 'in the top right', etc.

- consider the impacts or future actions of what you can see; for example, the impacts of flooding on an environment.

> **Tip** Consider drawing circles directly onto a photo to pick out the main features.

Activity 7

Study **Figure 4**, a photo showing urban greening in Singapore. Use arrows or circles to add the following labels to **Figure 4**:

(a) Crops grown on a rooftop.

(b) Trees planted on pavements and open spaces.

Figure 4

6. Learn and use your examples and case studies

What are 'examples' and 'case studies'?

- **Examples:** these are real-world studies that usually focus on a single event or location. In Paper 1 you are required to study an example of a tectonic hazard and a tropical storm. In Paper 2, you are required to study an example of an urban regeneration project and tourism in an LIC/NEE. These are places that an examiner can reasonably ask you to include in an answer.

- **Case studies:** these are broader real-world studies, for example, studying a city such as Rio de Janeiro or a country such as Nigeria. An examiner can expect you to know about particular projects in that city, such as housing or water projects, and the names of districts.

It is really important to learn and refer to your examples and case studies when asked to do so in the exams. This level of supportive detail will affect the level you achieve. A revision checklist for you to complete and refer to is provided on page 112.

7. Write to the space and time available

Space

- Exam papers give you **2 lines per mark**. So, for a 2-mark question, you will have 4 lines to write your answer.

- You will be given extra lines for 4-, 6- and 9-mark questions. Beyond this, you can use supplementary sheets provided in the exam room.

- Be precise and concise in your answers and try to stick to the lines available.

Time

You have roughly **1 minute per mark**. Watch your timing very carefully to avoid running out of time and losing marks.

> **Tip** Try to learn about four specific facts or figures for each example/case study. Examples and case studies are most likely to be required in 6- or 9-mark questions.

> **Tip** Try to support a statement by referring to a place or an event if you can. For example, 'such as the M25' or 'e.g. Mount Etna'. You should try to use exemplars (references to a place or event) whenever you can. Don't invent information.

 **Activity 8**

Look at the answer to the following exam question. It is too long and the student has wasted time waffling. Highlight or underline parts of the answer that could have been left out.

Figure 5

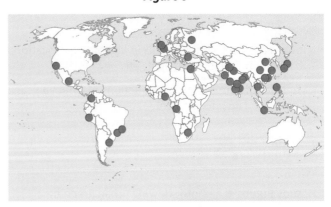

> Study **Figure 5**, a map showing the predicted locations of megacities in 2030. Using **Figure 5** and your own knowledge, describe the distribution of megacities in 2030. **[4 marks]**

Figure 5 shows the location of megacities in the world in 2030. Megacities are located all over the world. They are concentrated particularly in Asia, for example in India and China. There are lots of megacities in China. There are few megacities in Africa – only three. Elsewhere, there are some megacities in Europe and in North and South America. A lot of megacities are located on the coast. This is because they are ports and have developed as trading centres. So, as the map shows, there are lots of megacities all over the world.

> **Tip** Make a simple plan (in the margin) before starting to answer 6- and 9-mark questions. Write a list or draw a simple spider diagram.

8. Think (plan) before you write

The time allocated to each question takes account of your need to **observe**, **interpret**, **think** and **plan**. So, for a 4-mark question, you should use up to 1 minute for thinking and planning and about 3 minutes for writing.

9. Check your answers

Ideally, you should have a few minutes left at the end of the exam. However well you think you have done, it is extremely unlikely that you have scored 100%! If you have time, methodically check your answers, especially the shorter, more factual answers:

- Double-check answers to multiple-choice questions.

- Make sure all diagrams are complete.

- Check calculations and that measurement units are included.

Then look at the higher-mark questions and make sure you have followed all the instructions precisely.

 **Activity 9**

Study **Figure 6**, a graph showing economic sectors in selected countries. Look at the following answers to exam questions based on **Figure 6**. They contain careless mistakes that could cost marks. Can you spot and correct the mistakes?

(a) State the size in per cent of the UK's tertiary sector. **[1 mark]**

_____ *80* _____

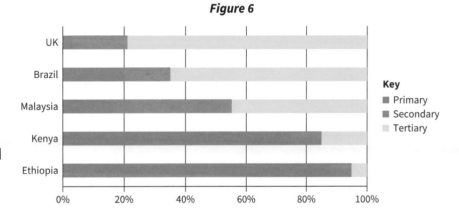

Figure 6

Key
■ Primary
■ Secondary
□ Tertiary

(b) Compare the economic sectors between Malaysia and Ethiopia. **[3 marks]**

Malaysia has a much smaller primary sector than Ethiopia (about 7% compared to about 85%). However, Malaysia has much larger secondary and primary sectors than Ethiopia. Malaysia's secondary sector (about 40%) is larger than Ethiopia's (about 7%) and its tertiary sector (64%) is larger than Ethiopia's (about 6%).

10. Look after yourself!

You need to be at your best when you sit your exams.

- Structure and plan your revision well in advance. Revise in intensive 40-minute sessions and take a complete break between each one.

- Try to exercise regularly. It's good for the body and the mind!

- Eat well and drink water regularly. Don't skip breakfast on exam day: food is mind fuel!

- Get plenty of sleep and put social media 'on hold'.

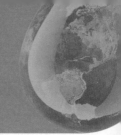

Getting to grips with...

Social, economic and environmental factors

Paper 1	Paper 2	Paper 3
• Extreme weather in the UK • River landforms – flood management scheme • Glacial landforms – impacts of tourism	• Urban – case study of LIC/NEE city • Urban – case study of UK city • Economic – case study of LIC/NEE • Economic futures in the UK • Resources in the UK	• Section A – issue evaluation (especially the decision-making question)

What are social, economic and environmental factors?

It's often useful to group together different aspects of geography. You will find that the terms '**social**', '**economic**' and '**environmental**' are widely used across the specification and in the exams. You need to have a clear understanding of their meaning.

Social – this applies to people and people's behaviour (e.g. jobs, education, health, recreation).

Economic – this is to do with money (e.g. the cost of building roads and railways, or repairing an area struck by an earthquake).

Environmental – this applies to the environment (e.g. pollution, ecosystems, climate change).

> 💡 **Tip** If you are instructed to write about only one factor in an exam question, such as 'economic factors', you will gain no credit if you write about other factors.

> 💡 **Tip** Consider using the headings of 'social', 'economic' and 'environment' to organise your revision notes. You could also use these terms to provide a framework for an exam answer.

(a) Decide if the following effects of Typhoon Haiyan (2013) are social, economic or environmental. Note that some may be more than one type. Two have been done for you.

Effects of Typhoon Haiyan (2013)	Type of effect (tick one or more boxes)		
	Social	Economic	Environmental
About 6300 people killed	✓		
600 000 people displaced			
Power lines and crops destroyed			
Tacloban airport terminal badly damaged			
6 million people lost their source of income		✓	
Looting and violence broke out			
Coast strewn with debris			
Shortages of food and water led to outbreaks of disease			
Water sources polluted by seawater and sewage			
Many hospital, schools and shops destroyed			
Loss of jobs			

(b) Widespread flooding from the typhoon caused landslides and blocked roads. Suggest **one** economic and **one** environmental effect of the flooding.

Social	Economic	Environmental
Blocked roads would have made it difficult for people to receive aid in the form of water, food and medicines.		

 **Activity 2**

Look at **Figure 1**, an aerial photo of Cambridge Science Park. The science park is the triangular area of land in the centre of the photo bounded by three main roads.

(a) The factors below explain why this is a good location for a science park. Identify whether they are social (S), economic (Ec) or environmental (En) factors.

Figure 1

- Open green spaces make this a pleasant place to work.

  _____

- Land on the edge of Cambridge is cheaper than in the centre. _____

- There is good road access for the transport of people, goods and services. _____

- There are opportunities (grass and footpaths) for recreation and fitness. _____

- Nearby housing provides homes for workers. _____

- Low-rise, high-tech buildings produce low levels of carbon emissions (lack of chimneys). _____

(b) Use arrows to locate the factors in part **(a)** on the photo, where possible.

Now try this!

Using **Figure 1** above, suggest the economic and environmental advantages of the location of Cambridge Science Park.

[4 marks]

_____

_____

_____

_____

_____

_____

_____

_____

📝 **Tip**
Refer to economic and environmental evidence from Figure 1. Make sure you explain how each factor is a locational advantage.

Geographical scale

Understanding scale

There are two types of scale: **spatial scale** and **temporal scale**.

Spatial scale

Spatial scale refers to 'space'.

- *Local* scale: the smallest spatial area, e.g. a freshwater pond.
- *Regional* scale: this may be a region within national boundaries (e.g. the south-west of the UK) or one that crosses national boundaries (e.g. the Sahara Desert).
- *National* scale: a country (e.g. Brazil).
- *Global* scale: the largest spatial scale, involving vast areas (e.g. global ecosystems, such as tropical rainforests or tundra).

(AQA) Specification links

Paper 1	Paper 2	Paper 3
• Tectonic hazards • Weather hazards • Climate change • Living world	• Urban issues and challenges • Changing economic world • Resources	• Section A – issue evaluation

Activity 1

(a) State whether the following are at the local, regional, national or global scale. Write 'L', 'R', 'N' or 'G' next to each one.

- Freshwater pond _____
- Middle East _____
- Sahara Desert _____

- Tropical rainforest _____
- Town centre _____
- Climate change _____

(b) Identify and write **one** more example for each of local, regional and global scales.

- Local: _____
- Regional: _____
- Global: _____

Temporal scale

Temporal scale refers to 'time'. For example, it is possible to consider **short-term** (hours/days) and **long-term** (weeks/months) effects of an earthquake.

Activity 2

Look at the table below. It identifies short-term and long-term effects of an earthquake.

Short-term effects	Long-term effects
• Buildings collapse • People are killed or injured	• Damage to businesses result in falling incomes • Children's education suffers if schools destroyed

- Electricity is cut off
- Poor conditions may lead to disease

- Some people migrate to safer areas
- People need water, food, shelter and medicine

Decide whether the above effects are long-term or short-term and link them with arrows to the correct boxes.

> **Tip** Try to refer to scale – both spatial and temporal – when answering 4-, 6- and 9-mark questions. It gives you a chance to offer different points of view.

Worked example

Suggest the effects of road building in a tropical rainforest. **[4 marks]**

Road building in the Amazon may have serious **short-term** effects on **local** communities, such as taking away their food supply. However, it could bring **long-term** benefits (e.g. tourism) at both the **local** (e.g. jobs in construction or within hotels) and **national** scale (e.g. increased taxes to be spent on improving healthcare and education). However, deforestation may have harmful **global** consequences by increasing carbon emissions.

Examiner feedback

This answer reaches Level 2 and is awarded the full 4 marks because it:

- focuses on positive and negative effects, with clear examples of both
- makes good use of various scales (in bold) to develop the discussion.

💡 **Tip**
When reading a graph (e.g. a graph of global population growth), use a ruler to accurately read from the x-axis (horizontal) and y-axis (vertical).

Scale warnings!

Be careful when using scale. Potential 'banana skin' topics include:

Climate change

- Graphs may show trends over hundreds or thousands of years so be very careful when reading the axes.
- A **short-term** individual weather event does not, on its own, provide evidence for **longer-term** climate change.

Landscapes

Remember that the formation of landscapes is generally extremely slow, involving hundreds or thousands of years.

UK city and LIC/NEE country

In an exam, only write about the spatial scale given in the question.

Development

Development indicators (e.g. GNI) can be misleading as there can be huge extremes of wealth within a country.

For example, Nigeria has quite a high level of development but at the local scale (e.g. in squatter settlements) there is a lot of poverty.

Now try this!

Study **Figure 1**, a photo showing earthquake and tsunami damage in Pau, Indonesia in 2018.
Using **Figure 1**, suggest the immediate responses to the natural hazard shown.   **[4 marks]**

Figure 1

💡 **Tip**
Remember, you must refer to the photo to reach Level 2. Start your answer with 'Figure 1 shows…'. Make sure you stick to 'immediate' (short-term) responses.

_____

_____

_____

_____

_____

_____

_____

_____

Sustainability and sustainable development

What is sustainability?

In geography, 'sustainable' is used to indicate that an action or plan is designed to be long-lasting and have a minimal negative effect on people and the environment. For example, sustainable river management involves soft engineering schemes, such as tree planting and the creation of wetlands.

Sustainable development

Sustainable development is all about long-term improvements in people's quality of life, which also has minimal (if any) harmful impacts on the environment. For example, a small-scale hydro scheme can provide huge long-term benefits to the local community with few, if any, harmful impacts on the environment.

Sustainable development is not just about the environment. For example, Fairtrade's sustainable development projects are embedded within local communities, helping to increase food production, increase incomes and improve people's quality of life.

AQA **Specification links**

Paper 1	Paper 2	Paper 3
• Tropical rainforest management	• Urban sustainability • UK economic futures (modern industrial developments) • Resources	• Section A – issue evaluation

Figure 1

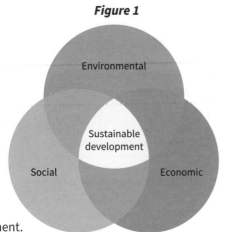

Activity 1

Look at **Figure 1**, a diagram showing the concept of sustainable development.

Decide if the following benefits of sustainable development are social (S), economic (Ec) or environmental (En). Write 'S', 'Ec' or 'En' after each one.

(a) More job opportunities _____

(b) Improved services (healthcare and education)

_____

(c) Increased incomes _____

(d) Increased food supply _____

(e) Trees planted _____

(f) Ecosystems preserved _____

(g) Less migration away from the area _____

(h) Tourism brings money into the area _____

Figure 2

Activity 2

Look at **Figure 2**, which shows some features of sustainable urban living. Use labels to identify features of sustainable urban living. One has been done for you.

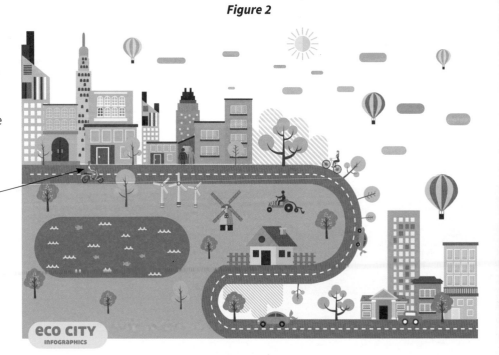

Use of bicycles

eco CITY
INFOGRAPHICS

Worked example

Study **Figure 3**, a photo showing ecotourism in Kibale National Park in Uganda. Using **Figure 3**, suggest how ecotourism can support the sustainable management of tropical rainforests. **[4 marks]**

Figure 3

> Answer focuses on ecotourism and makes good links with sustainable management

> Direct reference to the figure at the start

> Considers sustainability in a broad sense (environmental and economic)

Figure 3 shows a small group of tourists in a rainforest. This is a good example of sustainable management because it has minimal effects on the natural environment. In the photo, the tourists walk on a raised boardwalk to avoid trampling the forest floor. The boardwalk takes a narrow route between the trees, avoiding the need to cut down trees. This is a good example of sustainable management as it preserves wildlife habitats. The boardwalk is probably made from local wood providing jobs for local people. Local people may improve their incomes from ecotourism by acting as guides, building hotels and selling crafts.

Now try this!

For **one** of food, water or energy, explain how different strategies can be used to make supplies more sustainable. **[6 marks]**

_____

_____

_____

_____

_____

_____

_____

_____

_____

_____

_____

_____

Development

What is global development?

The term '**development**' is often applied to people's quality of life: their social and economic wellbeing. It is possible to divide the world into three broad development categories:

- **HICs:** high-income countries, which have a high level of social and economic development, where people enjoy a high quality of life (e.g. UK, USA, Japan, Australia and much of Europe).
- **NEEs:** newly emerging economies, which are developing rapidly and showing improvements in social and economic wellbeing (e.g. India, China, Nigeria and Brazil).
- **LICs:** low-income countries, which experience low levels of development and tend to rely on agriculture (e.g. African countries such as Sudan and Ethiopia).

AQA Specification links

Paper 1	Paper 2	Paper 3
• Tectonic hazards (contrasting levels of wealth)	• Urban issues and challenges (urbanisation, LIC/NEE case study) • Changing economic world (measuring development, demographic transition model, tourism, LIC/NEE case study) • Resources	• Section A – issue evaluation

The development gap

The term '**development gap**' describes the gap between rich and poor. This can apply at several different scales: globally, regionally (say within Africa) and within individual countries (such as Nigeria) and cities (such as Lagos).

Activity 1

The table below shows strategies used to reduce the development gap. Use your textbook or revision notes to add a second point in each of the boxes on the right. Try to refer to examples of projects and/or countries.

Strategy	How it reduces the development gap
Investment	• China has invested billions of dollars in Africa, helping to build new roads, bridges and sports stadiums
Tourism	• Money generated can be spent on transport, health and education
Aid	• Local aid projects provide health centres and improvements to services, such as water

Activity 2

Figure 1 shows the Demographic Transition Model (DTM).

(a) Label the two lines that show birth rate and death rate on the diagram.

(b) Shade and label the part of the graph that shows natural increase.

(c) Label the arrow at the base of the graph 'Increasing levels of development'.

Figure 1

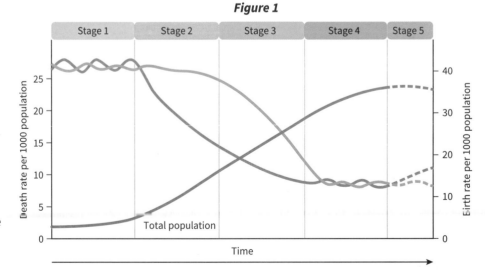

(d) Suggest why LICs often experience relatively high birth rates and death rates.

_____

_____

_____

_____

Activity 3

Look at **Figure 2**. It shows a coastal tourist development – a swimming pool in Rick's Cafe in Negril, Jamaica.

Add labels to identify the following evidence that tourism is helping to reduce the development gap.

(a) Construction of buildings creates jobs

(b) Swimming pool maintenance provides jobs for local people

(c) Local people can be tourist guides

(d) Local food used in cafes supports farmers' incomes

Figure 2

Now try this!

Using **Figure 2**, explain how tourism can help to reduce the development gap.   [4 marks]

_____

_____

_____

_____

_____

_____

_____

_____

What links, connections and interrelationships are there in geography?

Specification links

Synoptic links can be made across and within the topics of the specification.

Geography covers a wide range of different themes and subjects. You need to understand the links and connections between these different aspects.

- A **causal connection** is where an event (such as an earthquake) leads to an effect (such as a building collapsing).
- An **interrelationship** is where several factors affect each other or lead to an outcome, such as nutrient recycling in a tropical rainforest or the development of a tropical storm.

In the exam, you will be able to access the higher levels if you refer to connections and interrelationships.

Activity 1

Use lines to connect the causes and their effects in the two columns opposite.
One has been done for you.

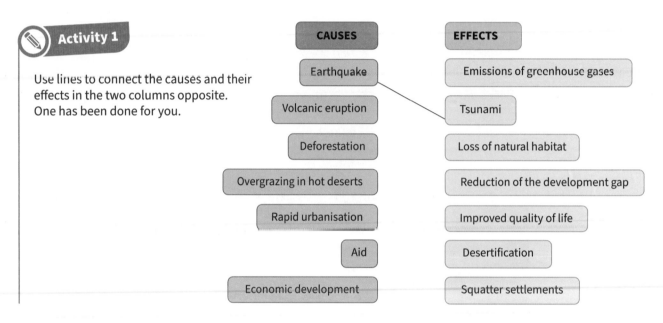

Activity 2

Here are some examples of 4-mark exam questions requiring you to make connections.

Use circles and connecting lines to identify the connections in each question. The first one has been done for you.

Explain how extreme weather in the UK can have economic impacts. **[4 marks]**

(a) Explain how plants and animals have adapted to the conditions in a hot desert (or cold environment). **[4 marks]**

(b) Explain how hard engineering structures can reduce the impacts of river flooding. **[4 marks]**

(c) Explain how urban regeneration can help to solve problems in urban areas. **[4 marks]**

Tip
Notice that all the questions in Activity 2 have the command word 'explain'. The examiner wants you to explain (give reasons for) the cause and effect relationship. These kinds of questions are extremely common – look out for them and make sure you make the link!

Worked example

Explain how physical factors can lead to uneven development. **[4 marks]**

The physical geography of a country can make development difficult. For example, some of Africa's poorest countries (e.g. Sudan) are landlocked, with no access to the sea for trade. In the tropics, countries may suffer from pests and diseases, causing food shortages. Extreme weather such as droughts and floods can cause damage (e.g. to roads) and hardship to people, especially in parts of Africa.

Examiner feedback

This answer reaches Level 2 and gains 4 marks because:

- the answer focuses on physical geography only
- there is a good selection of physical geography factors (landlocked, pests/diseases, extreme weather)
- appropriate references are made to Africa.

Activity 3

Figure 1

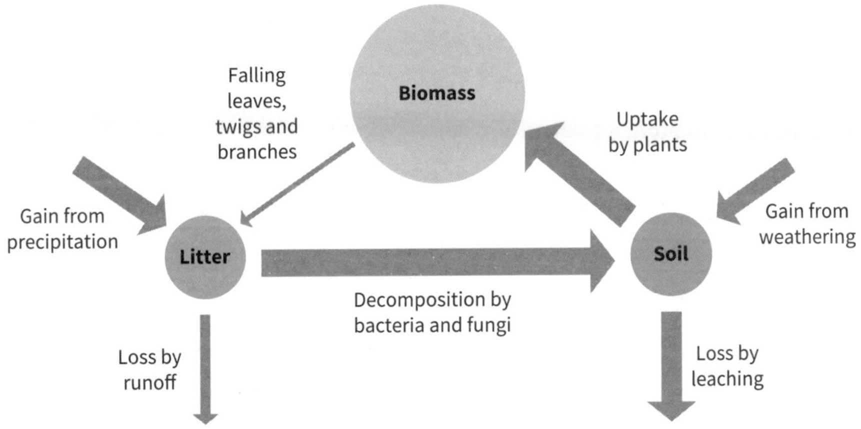

Look at **Figure 1**. It shows how nutrients (plant food) are being constantly recycled in a tropical rainforest. This is a great example of interrelationships.

- The circles are nutrient 'stores'. The larger the circle, the greater the amount of nutrients stored.
- The arrows are nutrient transfers. The wider the arrow, the greater the quantity of nutrient transfer.

(a) The largest store of nutrients is biomass. True or false? _____

(b) How are nutrients transferred from litter to soil?

_____

(c) Highlight the labels that are linked to the **climate**.

(d) Suggest how the nutrient cycle will be affected by deforestation.

_____

 Tip When answering an exam question, always try to refer to a range of relevant factors. Consider the importance of interrelationships between the factors (does one influence another?)

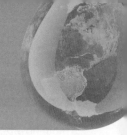

Upgrade your topic knowledge
1 The challenge of natural hazards

Tectonic hazards: physical processes at plate margins

The Earth's crust is made up of a number of huge slabs of solid rock called tectonic **plates**. Deep within the Earth, vast currents of heat (**convection currents**) cause the plates to move against each other at the plate margins, which causes earthquakes and/or volcanic activity.

💡 **Tip** The specification requires you to understand the processes at plate margins and link these processes to earthquakes and volcanic activity.

Plate margin	Earthquakes	Volcanic activity
Constructive (two plates moving **away** from each other)	Rising magma fractures rocks near the surface, causing them to crack and snap. This causes earthquakes.	The rising magma reaches the surface, resulting in a volcanic eruption.
Destructive (two plates moving **towards** each other)	As one plate tries to slide beneath the other, pressure builds up. Release of pressure causes an earthquake.	As one plate slides beneath the other it melts, creating magma that rises to the surface to form volcanic eruptions.
Conservative (two plates sliding **alongside** each other)	Pressure builds up as two plates try to slide alongside each other. Release of pressure causes an earthquake.	There is no magma so there are no volcanic eruptions.

 **Activity 1**

Figure 1 shows the three main types of plate margin.

(a) Use the information in the table above to label each diagram.

(b) Add the label 'volcano' where appropriate in **Figure 1**.

(c) Why do earthquakes occur at plate margins?

_____

_____

(d) Why are there volcanoes at constructive plate margins?

_____

(e) Why are there no volcanoes at conservative plate margins?

_____

Figure 1

Plate margin: _____

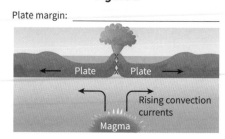

Plate margin: _____

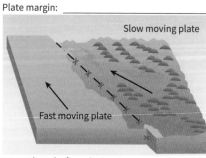

Plate margin: _____

x = earthquake focus/epicentre

Climate change: the greenhouse effect

The **greenhouse effect** is a natural blanket of atmospheric warmth. Without it, it would be too cold for life to exist on Earth!

Human activities, such as burning fossil fuels, have led to a large increase in the concentration of greenhouse gases in the atmosphere – especially carbon dioxide. This has resulted in higher temperatures, leading to global warming and climate change. This is the **enhanced greenhouse effect**, which is explained in **Figure 2**.

Climate change is already having dramatic effects on our weather – there are more frequent and extreme events such as floods, droughts and wildfires. Sea levels are rising as ice sheets melt and oceans become warmer.

Tip

Remember that the greenhouse effect is a natural process. **Higher** global temperatures are explained by the **increase** in the emissions of greenhouse gases by human activities, which has **increased** (enhanced) the greenhouse effect.

Figure 2

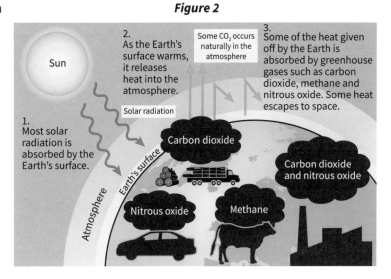

Activity 2

Use **Figure 2** to complete the gaps.

Heat energy from the sun is called _____ radiation. It warms up the surface of

the _____. Rising heat is absorbed in the atmosphere by _____ gases,

such as _____ dioxide and methane. Some heat escapes to _____.

Human activities, such as _____ and _____, have increased the

emission of greenhouse gases. This has increased the greenhouse _____ resulting

in higher _____ on Earth.

Now try this!

Study **Figure 3**, which shows carbon dioxide in the atmosphere (1750–2010) measured in parts per million (ppm)

Figure 3

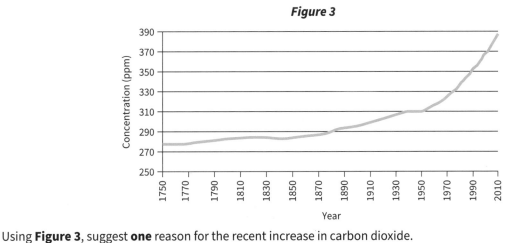

Using **Figure 3**, suggest **one** reason for the recent increase in carbon dioxide.　　　　　　**[2 marks]**

_____

_____

_____

_____

Ecosystems

An **ecosystem** is a natural system made up of living organisms (plants, animals, bacteria, etc.) and the natural environment. Ecosystems can be identified at the local scale (e.g. freshwater pond) and at the global scale (e.g. tropical rainforest), where they are called **biomes**.

Activity 1

Figure 1 identifies the community of living organisms in a deciduous woodland ecosystem.

Add the following labels to identify key features of the ecosystem:

(a) Climate (temperature and rainfall)

(b) Soil

(c) Primary producer (e.g. grass, leaves) converting the sun's energy by photosynthesis

(d) Primary consumer (e.g. rabbit)

(e) Secondary consumer (e.g. fox)

(f) Decomposer (e.g. fungi, bacteria)

Figure 1

Interrelationships

Ecosystems at all scales involve complex **interrelationships** (links) between biotic (living) and abiotic (environmental, non-living) components, for example between producers and consumers.

Interdependence

Components of an ecosystem are **interdependent** – they depend on one another for their survival. For example, plants depend on the soil for water and nutrients (plant food). In turn, the soil's fertility depends on the decomposition of organic matter, such as leaves (see **Figure 1** on page 23).

Interdependence explains why change can have huge impacts on an ecosystem. For example, draining a freshwater pond causes some plants to die and others to thrive, which changes habitats and affects the types and numbers of insects and animals.

> **Tip** Try to use the terms 'interrelationships' and 'interdependence' when answering exam questions on ecosystems. They will help you to achieve higher levels.

Activity 2

Figure 2 shows interrelationships (food web) in a tropical rainforest. It uses arrows to show who is eating whom!

(a) Define 'food web'.

_____

(b) Name **two** primary consumers.

_____

(c) Imagine that a disease wipes out the agouti. Suggest **two** ways that this may affect the ecosystem.

_____

_____

Figure 2

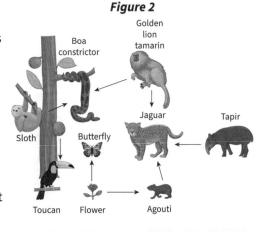

Biodiversity

Biodiversity describes the variety of life in an ecosystem or global biome. High biodiversity is a feature of a healthy, sustainable ecosystem.

In some ecosystems, biodiversity is being lost by people's direct actions (e.g. deforestation) or indirect actions (e.g. climate change). In tropical rainforests, deforestation reduces biodiversity, leading to many species of plants and animals becoming endangered or even extinct.

 **Activity 3**

Figure 3 shows deforestation in Laos, South-East Asia.

Figure 3

(a) How is the man clearing the forest?

_____

(b) Describe the land in the foreground.

_____

(c) Annotate the photo to identify these **three** likely effects on biodiversity:

- Reduction in variety of plants/trees, destroying habitats and reducing biodiversity.
- Grasses dominate the ground, restricting biodiversity.
- Fire may kill some animals or drive them away from the area.

Now try this!

Study **Figure 4**, which shows threats to tropical rainforests

Figure 4

Approximately 17% of the Amazon rainforest has been cleared, mostly for cattle ranching.

Logging causes loss of biodiversity, species extinction, flooding, and reduces the ability of trees to absorb carbon emissions.

THREATS
to tropical rainforests

Mining causes deforestation and pollution. Vegetation is cleared and the quality of the local food and water supply is damaged.

In countries like Indonesia, palm oil production has diminished the local orang-utan population by as much as 50%.

Using **Figure 4**, outline **two** causes for the loss of biodiversity in tropical rainforests.   **[2 marks]**

_____

_____

_____

_____

Physical processes

When describing the formation of landforms, you need to write about the physical processes involved. Use the correct terminology and show that you understand each process.

Weathering: the disintegration or decay of rocks. Chemical weathering involves a chemical change that is usually associated with water. Mechanical (physical) weathering involves rocks breaking apart physically, with no chemical change.

Mass movement: the downhill movement of weathered material under the force of gravity.

Erosion: the wearing away and removal of material by a moving force, such as a breaking wave.

Deposition: when transported material is dropped, usually when there is a fall in velocity (e.g. at the inside bend of a river meander).

Transportation: the movement of eroded material, carried by the sea, a river or a glacier.

 **Activity 1**

For the two landscapes you have studied, draw linking lines to match the physical processes with their correct definitions.

COASTAL/RIVER LANDSCAPES

Hydraulic action (power)	Rocks carried by the sea or in a river are used to carry out erosion
Abrasion	Material is rolled along the sea/river bed
Attrition	Erosion: dissolving of rocks or minerals Transportation: transport of dissolved chemicals in the water
Solution	Rocks smash together and break into smaller and smoother particles
Traction	The power of water erodes the cliff or bed and banks of a river

GLACIAL LANDSCAPES

Freeze-thaw weathering	Slippage of ice along a curved surface
Abrasion	Loose rocks are 'plucked' from solid bedrock as meltwater freezes them to the base of a glacier
Plucking	Rocks carried beneath a glacier grind away the underlying bedrock (like sandpaper)
Rotational slip	Repeated cycles of freezing and thawing, enlarging cracks and causing rocks to break away
Bulldozing	The snout of an advancing glacier pushes deposited sediment

Sequence of a landform formation

When writing about the formation of a landform, it's important to get the order (sequence) right. This shows that you clearly understand what is happening.

Tip Write a plan using numbers (1, 2, 3 and so on) to make sure that you have the correct sequence of events. Then use simple annotated diagrams/sketches to describe the sequence of events. It is the labelling/annotation that is important, not the quality of the sketch.

 **Activity 2**

Figure 1 shows the formation of an ox-bow lake. The four diagrams have been mixed up. Write numbers 1, 2, 3 and 4 above the diagrams to put them in their correct order.

Figure 1

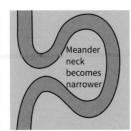 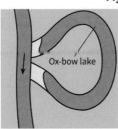 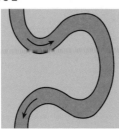 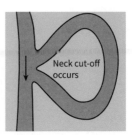

Worked example

Using **Figure 1**, explain the formation of an ox-bow lake. **[4 marks]**

Figure 1 shows that an ox-bow lake is an old river meander that has been cut off. In a meander, water flows fastest around the outside of the bend, causing erosion by the processes of hydraulic action and abrasion. Over time, the meander neck narrows (as shown on Figure 1) as opposite river banks are eroded. During a flood, the river will break through the meander neck to form a faster, straight channel (Figure 1). Figure 1 shows that slower water at the sides of the new channel causes deposition which blocks off the old meander. The cut-off meander is now an ox-bow lake.

✓ Examiner feedback

The answer gains Level 2 and all 4 marks.

- The answer refers to Figure 1.
- It shows a good understanding of processes (erosion, deposition).
- It states a clear sequence of events.
- It makes good use of geographical terminology.

Management strategies (coasts and rivers)

There are two types of strategy for managing the coast and preventing river flooding:

- **Hard engineering:** using artificial structures (such as a seawall) to control or prevent natural processes.
- **Soft engineering:** using strategies that work with natural processes and do not involve large, artificial structures.

When deciding which strategy to use, planners weigh up the costs and benefits.

Costs
• Hard engineering is very expensive
• Loss of habitats and damage to ecosystems
• Impact on the landscape and on people's views and access

Benefits
• Reduction of financial loss caused by cliff collapse or flood damage
• Improved facilities for people (e.g. promenade on a seawall)
• People feel safer

✎ Activity 3

The sketches in **Figure 2** illustrate some hard- and soft-engineering strategies to prevent river flooding.

Figure 2

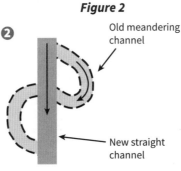
Old meandering channel
New straight channel

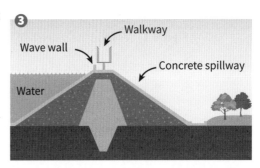
Walkway
Wave wall
Concrete spillway
Water

❶  Trees planted to INTERCEPT rainfall upstream so reduce river levels

(a) Name each strategy.

1 _____ 2 _____ 3 _____

(b) Identify if each one is hard or soft engineering.

1 _____ 2 _____ 3 _____

(c) Briefly describe how each one reduces the flood hazard.

1 _____

2 _____

3 _____

Describing global patterns of urban change

It is very likely that you will be asked to describe **distributions** and **patterns** on maps. In your descriptions, try to be very precise, referring to geographical locations and the data in the key.

What is urbanisation?

The term '**urbanisation**' describes the growth of urban areas by in-migration from rural areas and natural increase (births minus deaths). Today, urbanisation is almost static in HICs, which are already highly urbanised. However, in less urbanised LICs, urbanisation is rapid, putting a lot of pressure on housing, services and employment. This explains why squatter settlements are found in these cities.

 Tip Know the difference:

Distribution is where things are located. Identify dense and sparse concentrations with precise geographical locations.

A **pattern** is a regular distribution, for example one that forms lines (linear pattern) or radiates out from a central point (radial pattern).

 **Activity 1**

Look at **Figure 1**, a map of global patterns of urbanisation. Notice that rings have been drawn around the parts of the world with the highest levels of urbanisation. This technique helps you to describe patterns.

(a) Label the four ringed areas that have high values of urbanisation.

(b) Draw two rings to pick out the **low** values in much of Africa and South-East Asia.

(c) In a different colour, use rings to pick out any exceptions (anomalies) to the general patterns.

Figure 1

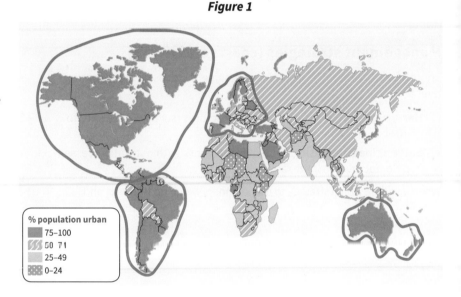

% population urban
- 75–100
- 50–74
- 25–49
- 0–24

Worked example

Using **Figure 1**, describe the pattern of urbanisation. **[4 marks]**

Figure 1 shows that there is a clear pattern of urbanisation. There are large areas with a relatively high level of urbanisation such as North and South America and Australia/New Zealand, where many countries are over 75% urbanised. Many countries in Europe and North Africa also have high rates of urbanisation, in excess of 50%. In contrast, much of Africa and South-East Asia are less than 50% urbanised. An exception to this pattern is Gabon in Africa (over 75%).

 Examiner feedback

This answer meets the criteria of Level 2 and earns all 4 marks.

- The answer starts with 'Figure 1 shows…', making immediate use of the figure (as instructed by the question).
- There is good use of the map with a clear focus on overall patterns.
- The answer is supported by the use of data in the key.

Describing urban growth

Urbanisation can be described using both maps and graphs. Maps like **Figure 1** show **spatial** patterns of urbanisation, whereas graphs like **Figure 2** describe **temporal** changes.

Activity 2

Figure 2 is a line graph showing the growth of Guangzhou, a city in China.

(a) Use the data in **Figure 2** to plot the projected population value for 2030 on the graph.

(b) By how much did the population grow between 1990 and 2015?

_____

(c) Describe the growth of Guangzhou from 1950 to 1990.

_____

(d) Describe the growth of Guangzhou from 1990 to 2030.

_____

(e) What is the evidence that Guangzhou is projected to grow faster than other cities in China and the world?

_____

_____

Figure 2

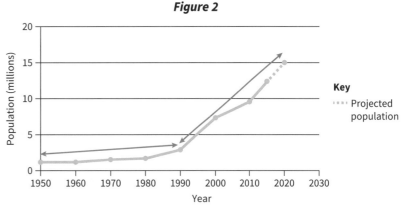

Year	1950	1990	2015	2030
Population (millions)	1.0	3.1	12.5	17.6
Global rank	71	63	20	16
National rank	7	7	4	3

> **Tip** Use arrows to pick out trends when describing a graph. This has been done on **Figure 2**.

Sustainable urban living

Figure 3 is a photo of Parc Central, a huge green space in the centre of Guangzhou, China. Guangzhou is striving to be a sustainable city. Sustainable strategies include:

- Encouraging cycling, walking and the use of public transport to reduce pollution.
- Creating green spaces for leisure; trees absorb carbon dioxide from the atmosphere.
- Designing buildings with solar panels and glass (sunlight reduces the need for electric lighting).
- Creating gardens to grow food for local people, which reduces food miles.
- Creating ponds, which prevents flooding and provides wildlife habitats.

Figure 3

Activity 3

Use annotations on **Figure 3** to identify and explain **four** sustainable living strategies in Guangzhou.

5 The changing economic world

What is economic development?

Economic development involves the growth of a region based on the creation of wealth. This might involve, for example, the development of farming, fishing or manufacturing industries. Wealth can be used to improve people's **quality of life** through education, public services and infrastructure. As a country's economy grows, so does quality of life for its people.

The multiplier effect

Look at **Figure 1**. It is a model of economic growth called the **multiplier effect**. It explains how economic development (e.g. the opening of a new factory) can lead to improvements in people's quality of life.

- New jobs mean workers need houses, schools and shops.
- Building materials are needed, and supply industries expand to create more jobs.
- Wages are used in the local economy and taxes help to improve services, education and healthcare.

Figure 1

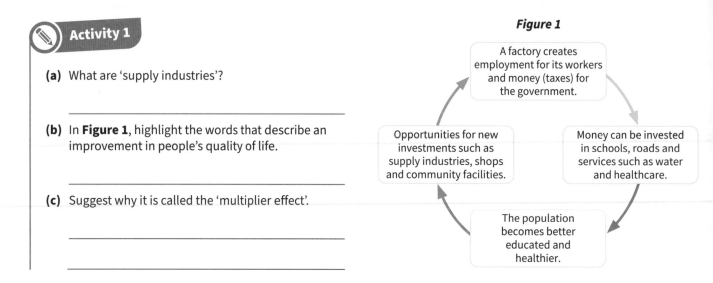

Activity 1

(a) What are 'supply industries'?

_____

(b) In **Figure 1**, highlight the words that describe an improvement in people's quality of life.

_____

(c) Suggest why it is called the 'multiplier effect'.

_____

_____

Activity 2

The table below lists economic developments in Nigeria following the discovery of oil. Place them in the correct order by writing 1 (the earliest to happen) to 5 (the most recent to happen) in the blank column.

Number (1–5)	The multiplier effect in Nigeria
	Oil workers needed houses, shops, schools, etc., which created further job opportunities in construction, retailing and services.
	The government spent money to improve people's quality of life (education, services, infrastructure).
	Oil was discovered in Nigeria in 1958. TNCs such as Shell invested money to extract oil.
	As an industrial country, Nigeria attracts investment from abroad and the multiplier effect continues.
	Oil extraction provided job opportunities to attract workers (over 65 000 now employed).

Tip Try to refer to the multiplier effect if it is appropriate to do so. It is a high-level concept and will help you to achieve a top mark.

Worked example

Explain how economic development can lead to improvements in people's quality of life. **[4 marks]**

Economic development can lead to improvements in people's quality of life through the multiplier effect. When a resource is exploited (such as oil in Nigeria) or a new factory is built, jobs are created in construction and in the factory. People have money to spend in shops, boosting the local economy and improving the quality of their lives. Supply industries expand, creating more jobs. Taxes provide money for the government to spend on improving services such as health, improving quality of life.

> Multiplier effect is clearly understood

> References a case study, which, although not required, is good practice

> Clear link between economic development and quality of life

Deindustrialisation in the UK

The multiplier effect can also work in reverse. This happened in the UK during the 1970s and 1980s when many old industries were forced to close, affecting local services and supply industries. Previously thriving regions became run down and derelict. This is called **deindustrialisation**.

Since then, the UK has become a **post-industrial economy**. Manufacturing has been largely replaced by the service sector (finance, construction and public services). Much of this growth has been driven by developments in information technology. The service sector now accounts for about 80 per cent of the UK's workforce.

Activity 3

Figure 2 shows a derelict industrial site in Brantham, UK.

Write the following labels on **Figure 2** to identify some of the problems of deindustrialisation.

(a) Factory has closed resulting in job losses.

(b) Land is derelict and unattractive.

(c) Land may contain hazardous materials.

(d) The area needs to be cleared before development.

Figure 2

Now try this!

Using **Figure 2** and your own understanding, suggest the impacts of deindustrialisation in the UK. **[4 marks]**

_____

_____

_____

_____

_____

_____

_____

_____

Understanding resource security and insecurity

There are a number of key terms that you need to understand:

- **Supply:** the availability or creation of resources.
- **Demand:** the use or consumption of resources by people.
- **Resource security:** when a country or region has access to enough food, water and energy to meet current and future demand. Resources could be home-produced or imported from safe and reliable (secure) sources abroad.
- **Resource insecurity:** when a country or region experiences shortages, and demand (consumption) exceeds supply.

Resource security in the UK

As an HIC, the UK enjoys reasonably high levels of resource security. It has high levels of self-sufficiency and strong trading links with the rest of the world to make up shortfalls in food and energy.

Activity 1

Figure 1 shows the threat to water security in the UK.

(a) Which colours indicate a high threat to water security?

_____

(b) Write one of the labels below on either side of the red line to describe the 'big picture' of water security in the UK.

- High threat to water security
- Low threat to water security

(c) Circle the following areas on the map:

- The area of highest threat in South East England
- The area with a relatively high level of threat in Scotland (Glasgow to Edinburgh)

(d) Complete the gaps in the following description of the pattern of water security in the UK. Choose words from the list below.

In the UK, there is a South East/_____ split in water security. In the South East there is

a _____ level of threat whereas in the North West there is a _____ level of threat.

The highest levels of threat are in the far South East (_____). The lowest levels of threat are in the

_____. One _____ is the central lowlands of Scotland (_____ to Edinburgh)

where there is a high level of threat.

| low | North West | Glasgow | anomaly | Scottish Highlands | high | Kent/Sussex |

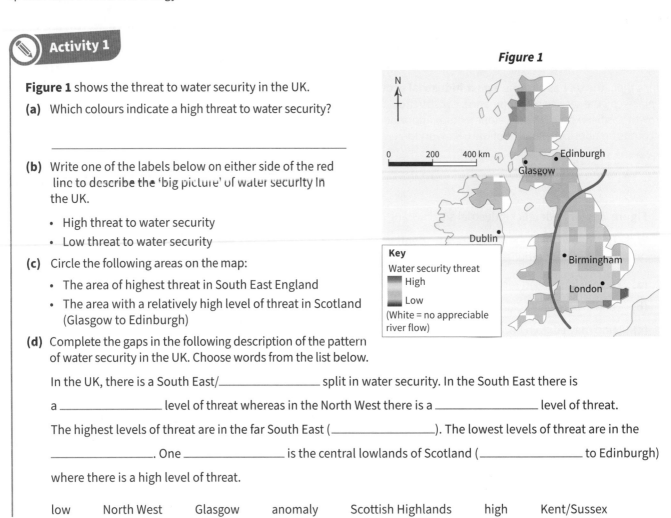

Figure 1

Key

Water security threat

High

Low

(White = no appreciable river flow)

Resource security and development

Globally, there is a link between resource security and development.

- Many LICs and some NEEs have **low** levels of resource security. They may have few natural resources and have to rely on expensive imports.
- Most HICs have **high** levels of resource security. Even if they have few natural resources, they can afford to import resources.

Activity 2

Tip When describing the effects of resource security or insecurity, consider social, economic and environmental factors. Also, try to consider positive and negative effects.

Country A (an HIC) has a high level of food security. Some of the effects on wellbeing are listed below.

(a) Sort the effects into **economic** and **social** ones. Write 'Ec' or 'S' after each one.

- Commercial food production and food processing raises tax money for the government. _____

- Most people are well fed and are able to lead healthy lives. _____

- Obesity has become a significant problem among children. _____

- Exporting surplus food provides money for the government. _____

(b) Highlight the one **negative** effect listed above.

Global water security

Look at **Figure 2**. It shows global water security by identifying areas of scarcity (areas in short supply). Notice that there are two types of water scarcity:

- **Physical** water scarcity: arid regions where there is a lack of water, such as deserts.
- **Economic** water scarcity: where water exists but it is too expensive to access.

Figure 2

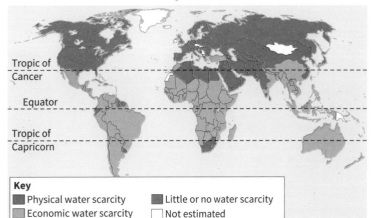

Key
- ■ Physical water scarcity
- ■ Economic water scarcity
- ■ Little or no water scarcity
- □ Not estimated

Activity 3

(a) Draw a line across the map to roughly split the 'Little or no water scarcity' regions (coloured blue) from the rest of the world.

(b) Africa suffers from water scarcity. True or false? _____

(c) Most of South America suffers from physical water scarcity. True or false? _____

(d) Suggest why North Africa suffers from physical water scarcity.

_____

_____

Tip When describing, don't use the word 'because'! 'Because' leads into a reason for something, which is not required in 'describe' questions.

Worked example

Using **Figure 2**, describe the pattern of global water scarcity. **[4 marks]**

Figure 2 shows that most of North America, Europe and northern Asia do not experience water scarcity – they have high levels of water security. Most regions experiencing physical water scarcity are located at the tropics and largely coincide with hot deserts, such as the Sahara. Within the tropics, most countries experience economic water scarcity (water insecurity). This includes much of Africa, South America and parts of southern Asia. There are one or two anomalies, for example Uruguay and Ecuador in South America do not experience water scarcity.

✓ Examiner feedback

This answer reaches Level 2 and gains the full 4 marks because it:

- focuses on describing patterns, making use of the lines of latitude
- makes frequent, accurate references to Figure 2 (countries and key), enabling access to the higher-level marks
- identifies some anomalies.

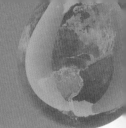

On your marks
Mopping up the 1-mark questions

Multiple-choice questions

The phrase 'multiple choice' in exam questions means exactly that – you are given a situation in which (usually) four possible answers are given, but only one is correct. That's your job – to find the correct answer! These questions are normally worth 1 mark where there's a choice of one from four possible answers.

What are the common mistakes?

Even top students often perform poorly on multiple-choice questions, throwing away important marks. Don't rush! They may only be worth 1 mark but this doesn't mean they're easy! Common mistakes include giving too many answers.

Tip Find the correct answer by crossing out the choices you **know** are wrong. That leaves one or two possible answers. This forces you to take your time choosing, making it more likely you'll get the correct answer.

Worked example

Study **Figure 1**, a graph showing variations in average temperature in Australia (1910–2018).

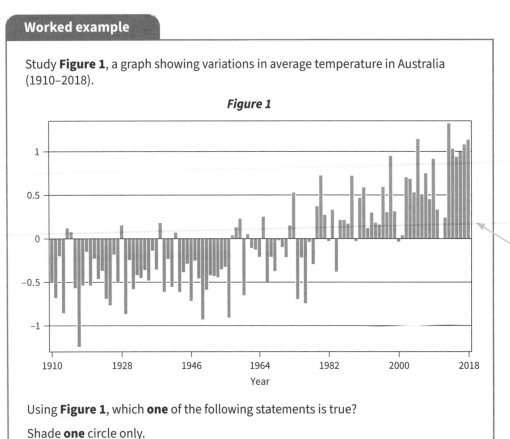

Figure 1

Using **Figure 1**, which **one** of the following statements is true?

Shade **one** circle only.

A Australia's temperatures were below average every year before 1946.

B Australia's temperatures showed a steady increase between 1982 and 2018.

C Australia's temperatures have been above the 1961–1990 average every year since 2001.

D Since 2000, Australia's temperatures have exceeded 0.5°C above the 1961-1990 average.

[1 mark]

This is the long-term average temperature. The blue bars show years where the average temperature was below the long-term average. The red bars show where the average temperature was above the long-term average.

Take time to look closely at both axes to make sure you understand the scales. Think about what's happening over time – what's the story?

Carefully work your way through the four options, looking closely at the graph. Try to identify the options that are definitely incorrect and draw a line through them. Take your time to make the correct decision. By elimination, you should be left with the correct answer.

Now try this!

1. Study **Figure 1**, which shows the tectonic plates in Iceland.

Figure 1

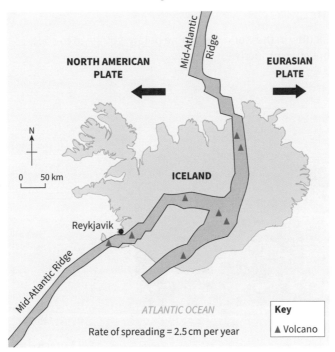

Using **Figure 1**, calculate how long it will take the plates to spread by 100 m.

Shade **one** circle only.

A 400 years

B 4000 years

C 2500 years

D 40 years

[1 mark]

2. Which term is best defined by the phrase 'the unplanned growth of urban areas into the surrounding countryside'?

Shade **one** circle only.

A Urbanisation

B Urban regeneration

C Urban greening

D Urban sprawl

[1 mark]

3. Which of the following best describes how sedimentary rocks are formed?

Shade **one** circle only.

A Formed from molten rock beneath the Earth's surface

B Formed from molten rock upon the Earth's surface

C Formed when earth movements occur

D Formed from material laid down by rivers, moving ice or the sea

[1 mark]

Skills questions

Skills are an important part of your Geography studies. They include interpreting resources such as maps, diagrams, graphs or tables of data. Your exams will feature a number of questions designed to test your ability to use them.

What are the common mistakes?

Skills-based questions vary in difficulty. In the worked example below, you need to spot evidence in order to answer the question properly.

Worked example

Figure 1

1. Name the landform at **A** in **Figure 1**.

   Stack   **[1 mark]**

2. Suggest one piece of evidence from **Figure 1** that this feature once formed part of a coastal arch.

                                                              [1 mark]

   There is debris between the stack and the mainland,
   which is the remains of an arch.

> Question 1 tests your knowledge. It just needs a one-word answer that names the landform.

> Question 2 needs some interpretation. You need to know what a coastal arch is. If you know that landform A is a stack, you'll know it formed when an arch collapsed. The rocks show the rubble from when it collapsed!

Now try this!

1. **Figure 1** shows how the ecosystem changes depending on the height above sea level.

   Figure 1

Height above sea level	Ecosystem
0–900 m	Tropical rainforest
900–1800 m	Temperate forest

   1.1. Using **Figure 1**, complete the line graph for tropical rainforest and temperate forest in **Figure 2**.

   [1 mark]

   Figure 2

   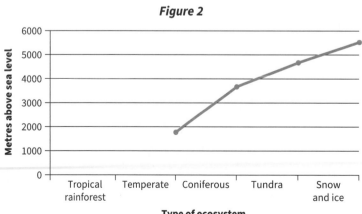

1.2. Complete the following sentence.

[1 mark]

Coniferous forest exists between _____ metres and _____ metres above sea level.

1.3. At what height does tundra give way to snow and ice?

[1 mark]

_____

2. Study **Figure 3**, a 1:50 000 Ordnance Survey map of Alnwick, a town in Northumberland. The scale is 2 cm = 1 km.

Figure 3

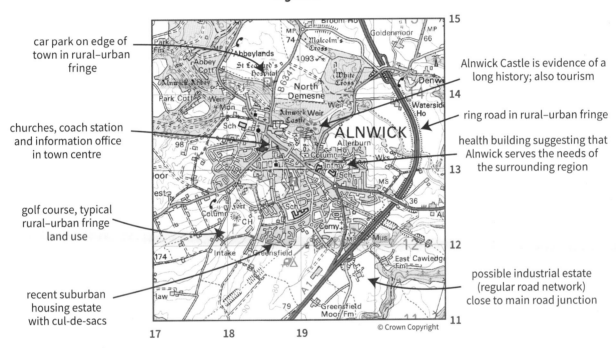

car park on edge of town in rural–urban fringe

churches, coach station and information office in town centre

golf course, typical rural–urban fringe land use

recent suburban housing estate with cul-de-sacs

Alnwick Castle is evidence of a long history; also tourism

ring road in rural–urban fringe

health building suggesting that Alnwick serves the needs of the surrounding region

possible industrial estate (regular road network) close to main road junction

© Crown Copyright

2.1. Using **Figure 3**, give the four-figure grid reference for the grid square that contains Alnwick Castle.

Shade **one** circle only.

A 1318 ◯

B 1813 ◯

C 1913 ◯

D 1714 ◯

[1 mark]

2.2. In which direction does Goldenmoor (2014) lie from Alnwick Castle?

[1 mark]

_____

2.3. Measure and give the distance of the route of the A1 (in km) east of Alnwick, from the southern edge of the map (189110) to the northern edge (198150). Give your answer to one decimal place.

[1 mark]

_____

Mopping up the 1-mark questions

Knowledge questions

'Knowledge' questions are simple questions that test you directly on what you know. Expect to see questions that ask you the meaning of key terms, or to select one of many terms that you have learned about.

What are the common mistakes?

These questions vary in difficulty – don't expect that they will be easy just because they are 'only' worth 1 mark.

- Basically, it comes down to whether you know the answer or not!

- Almost always, there is more than one way to give the answer, as the worked example below shows.

> **Tip** When revising, make a list of all the key words and phrases you need to know from the specification.
>
> When you answer a question, use the number of lines to guide how much you think you should write.
>
> - If one line is shown, only a word or brief phrase is expected.
> - If two lines are shown, a longer phrase or sentence is expected.

Worked example

1. Give the meaning of the term 'abiotic'.

[1 mark]

Things that don't include plants and animals in an ecosystem, such as water.

Only one answer line is given, so only a brief phrase is expected. Other possible answers to this question could include:

- 'non-living parts of an ecosystem' (or a food web)
- 'non-biotic', 'not biotic' or 'not biological'
- giving an example, such as 'rocks', 'minerals', 'water', 'soil'.

Now try this!

Try these questions. Time yourself – 4 minutes for all four questions!

1. Give **one** characteristic of a sedimentary rock.

[1 mark]

_____

2. Name **one** type of mechanical weathering that might have an impact on UK landscapes.

[1 mark]

_____

3. Farming is one example of a human activity affecting the landscape. Give **one** other example of a human activity that affects the landscape.

[1 mark]

_____

4. Give **one** natural cause of climate change.

[1 mark]

_____

Now try this!

Try these questions. A full sentence for each one is needed.

5. Give **one** piece of evidence that can be used to show natural climate change in the past.

[1 mark]

_____

_____

6. Give the meaning of the term 'counter-urbanisation'.

[1 mark]

_____

_____

7. Give the meaning of the initials 'HDI'.

[1 mark]

_____

_____

8. State **one** feature of a business park.

[1 mark]

_____

_____

9. State **one** primary effect of a tectonic hazard.

[1 mark]

_____

_____

10. Give the meaning of the term 'renewable energy'.

[1 mark]

_____

_____

11. Give the meaning of the word 'erosion'.

[1 mark]

_____

_____

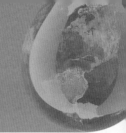

On your marks

Maxing out the 2-mark questions

How the 2-mark questions work

Sometimes examiners want you to describe or explain something in a little more detail. This means that you need to develop your answers with more detail in order to get the marks.

Look at this question:

> Rainforests are ecosystems. State **two** ways in which humans can protect ecosystems.　　　　　　　　　　　　　**[2 marks]**

There are **2** marks for this question, so you must suggest **two** ways of protecting ecosystems. You get 1 mark for each way or point that you give. The mark scheme tells examiners which ways they can mark as correct. It's just like the 1-mark questions, except you have to make two points!

Developing a 2-mark answer

The key to success is knowing how to turn 1 mark into 2. To achieve this, you need to learn how to **develop** answers. Consider the following question:

> Explain **one** possible economic impact of climate change.　　　　　　**[2 marks]**

In this case, it is not enough to just *name* one economic impact – this would earn just 1 mark. To earn 2 marks your answer must be either:

- **developed** (i.e. described with extra detail), or
- **exemplified** (i.e. giving an example of what you are describing).

Tip　To develop an answer, extend it using one of the following phrases:

- 'so that…'
- 'which means that…'
- 'which leads to…'
- 'therefore…'
- 'for example…'
- 'because…'

'Describe' and 'Explain'

Make sure that you know the difference between '**Describe**' and '**Explain**'.

'**Describe**' means you need to say what is there, what you see, or what something is like.

'**Explain**' means you need to say *how* or *why* something occurs.

Worked example

1. Describe one natural cause of climate change.　　　　　　**[2 marks]**

   Milankovitch cycles are a natural cause ✓ when the angle of the earth's axis changes. ✓

   - For 2-mark questions, you should extend the answer with what happens as a result, or with an example of how something occurs.

   > The cause is stated for 1 mark.

   > An additional detail is given for a second mark.

2. Explain one natural cause of climate change.　　　　　　**[2 marks]**

   Milankovitch cycles occur when the angle of the earth's axis changes ✓ because the earth's spin wobbles like a spinning top causing climate systems to change. ✓

   > A cause is stated for one mark.

   > The explanation is extended by using the word 'because'.

Now try this!

> **Tip** 'Describe' means to say what something is like, or what exists. So for question 1, think what life in a large developing world city is like, and simply say what it's like. For question 2, say what a tropical storm consists of. If you drew a diagram of it, what would you label?

1. Describe **one** feature of the quality of life in a major city in a low-income country (LIC) or newly emerging economy (NEE).

   [2 marks]

   _____

   _____

   _____

   _____

2. Describe **one** feature of the structure of a tropical storm.

   [2 marks]

   _____

   _____

   _____

   _____

> **Tip** 'Explain' means to give reasons why something is as it is or how it happens. So, for question 3, name the way in which economic development is measured and say *how* it does this. For question 4, say *why* a country might want investment, and why there might be benefits.

3. Explain **one** way in which economic development can be measured.

   [2 marks]

   _____

   _____

   _____

   _____

4. Explain **one** way in which high levels of investment could benefit an emerging country.

   [2 marks]

   _____

   _____

   _____

   _____

Skills questions

Many questions will ask you to look at a figure, such as a graph, map, photo or table, and then describe it. Figures like this usually contain data (i.e. numbers). These questions are testing your skills and ability to get information from the figure.

In questions like this, you could be asked to describe:

*   a change over time – known as a **trend** or **variation**
*   differences between places – a **pattern** or **distribution**.

You probably won't have seen the graph before, so you won't be asked to explain or give reasons in these questions.

Sometimes, the command word 'suggest' is used, because you can't be expected to know a particular example. But you can use intelligent guesswork to work out how or why something might happen.

Activity 1

Figure 1 shows mean global sea level to 2020, and a range of predictions about future changes by 2100.

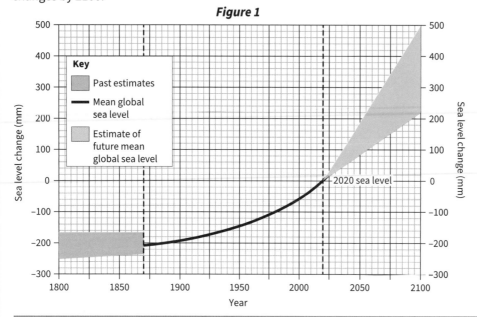

Describe the estimated future mean global sea level. **[2 marks]**

Now look at the answers below. Decide how many marks each answer earns, and give a reason.

Answer 1: Sea level is predicted to rise.

_____

_____

Answer 2: Sea level is predicted to rise. The predictions have a large range.

_____

_____

Answer 3: Sea levels are changing because the ice caps are melting.

_____

_____

Answer 4: Predicted increases have a wide range, from +200 to +500 mm by 2100.

_____

_____

> ### 💡 Tip
> If you are asked to describe a graph, look for these things:
>
> *   **The trend**. Is the data increasing or decreasing (or does it do both)?
> *   **The x-axis**. What are the years (or other units of time) over which the increase or decrease occurred?
> *   **The y-axis**. Give some figures to illustrate your answer. What was the value at the lowest point? Or at the highest point?
> *   **The range**. Calculate the difference between the highest and lowest points.

Now try this!

1. **Figure 1** shows a satellite photo of Hurricane Sandy off the coast of Florida, USA in 2012.

    Figure 1

    Using **Figure 1**, describe **one** feature of Hurricane Sandy.

    [2 marks]

    _____

    _____

    _____

    _____

    Figure 2

	Percentage of all journeys to work	
Journey time in minutes	**Megacity**	**Rest of the country**
1–15	50	82
16–30	20	8
31–45	15	6
46–1 hour	5	4
Over 1 hour	10	0

2. **Figure 2** shows the percentage of journey times to work for workers in a megacity in an NEE compared with the rest of the country.

    Describe **one** difference between journey times to work for people in the megacity and journey times for people in the rest of the country.

    [2 marks]

    _____

    _____

    _____

    _____

Knowledge questions

Questions that test your knowledge and understanding often ask for some detail.

- They need more detail than answers to 1-mark questions (see pages 36–41).

- This means that you need to develop your answers in the ways shown on pages 42–45.

- You would usually be asked to describe a feature or process, or explain a reason why something happens.

💡 **Tip**   Questions testing your knowledge usually have the following command words:

- '**Give**', e.g. 'Give one reason for the growth of megacities in NEEs'
- '**Describe**', e.g. 'Describe one landform in a river's upper course'
- '**Explain**', e.g. 'Explain one reason for the rapid growth of squatter settlements in megacities in NEEs'

Worked example

Study **Figure 1**, which shows the global atmospheric circulation.

Figure 1

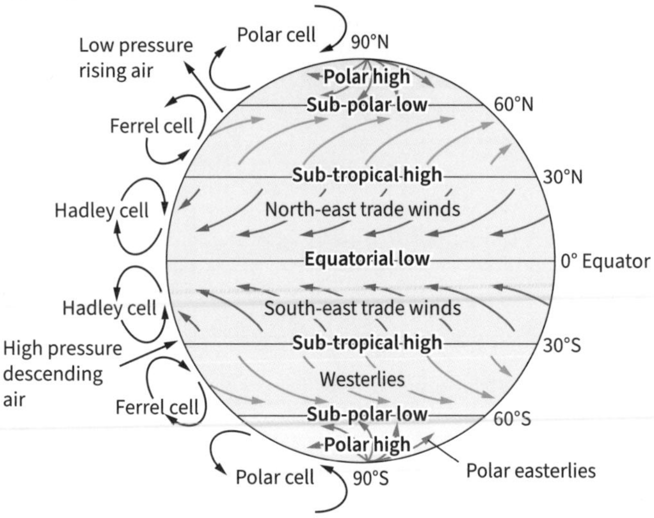

Polar cell — 90°N
Low pressure rising air
Polar high
Sub-polar low — 60°N
Ferrel cell
Sub-tropical high — 30°N
North-east trade winds
Hadley cell
Equatorial low — 0° Equator
Hadley cell
South-east trade winds
High pressure descending air
Sub-tropical high — 30°S
Westerlies
Ferrel cell
Sub-polar low — 60°S
Polar high
Polar cell — 90°S
Polar easterlies

Using **Figure 1**, explain **one** effect of global atmospheric circulation.

[2 marks]

Answer 1: *Global atmospheric circulation carries heat and moisture to other places* ✓*, e.g. the UK gets warmth from south-westerly winds from warm sub-tropical areas.* ✓

Answer 2: *Global atmospheric circulation forms currents of warm or cool air.* ✓

Answer 3: *Global atmospheric circulation forms winds,* ✓ *which heat up the North Atlantic and make it warmer than it would be without any current.* ✓

 Examiner feedback

Answer 1 is worth 2 marks. The candidate correctly says that global atmospheric circulation carries heat and moisture to other places. This is then **developed** by explaining the effect of south-westerly winds in the UK.

 Examiner feedback

Answer 2 is only worth 1 mark. The candidate has mentioned the currents of warm or cool air, but not what effect these have.

 Examiner feedback

Answer 3 is worth 2 marks. The candidate says what global atmospheric circulation does for 1 mark. Then this is **developed** with the example of how this heats the North Atlantic, gaining the second mark.

Now try this!

1. Describe **one** way in which a region affected by volcanic eruptions can prepare for this hazard.

   💡 **Tip** For a reminder of how to '**describe**', see page 43.

   [2 marks]

   _____

   _____

   _____

   _____

2. Describe **one** way in which large UK cities are trying to make transport more sustainable.

   [2 marks]

   _____

   _____

   _____

   _____

3. Explain **one** feature of a constructive plate margin.

   💡 **Tip** For a reminder of how to '**explain**', see page 43.

   [2 marks]

   _____

   _____

   _____

   _____

4. Explain **one** reason why low-income countries (LICs) often suffer worse impacts of tropical storms than high-income countries (HICs).

   [2 marks]

   _____

   _____

   _____

   _____

'Describe' and 'explain' questions

Students often mix up 'describe' and 'explain'.

- **Describe** means that you have to write an account of the main features of something (e.g. the main features of urban regeneration) or the steps in a process (e.g. how climate change occurs). Most 'describe' questions are worth 2 or 3 marks and so need to be developed. However, you don't have to give any reasons.

- **Explain** means that you have to give reasons for how or why something occurs (e.g. the causes of urban regeneration). You often have to give an example of something. You could even be asked to draw and label diagrams to support your explanation.

> **Tip** Make sure you are clear about the difference between 'describe' and 'explain':
> - **Describe:** tell it like it is, but don't give reasons why it is! Give information that paints a picture.
> - **Explain:** give reasons for how or why something happened.

Worked example

Think about this exam question. Look at the two answers below and make sure you understand why each one receives the marks it does.

Describe **one** feature of an urban regeneration project.

Answer 1:

East London's Queen Elizabeth Olympic Park has several sports venues which were designed to improve the economy of the area.

> 'Several sports venues' is a descriptive point, so earns the candidate 1 mark.

> 'which were designed to improve the economy of the area' is a reason for building them – so it's an explanation, not a description. This means this answer only receives 1 mark.

Answer 2:

East London's Queen Elizabeth Olympic Park has several sports venues, such as the London stadium.

> 'several sports venues' is a descriptive point, so earns the candidate 1 mark.

> The phrase 'such as the London stadium' is also descriptive – the candidate has used an example to develop the answer, which gets the second mark.

> **Tip** The word 'because' makes connections between cause and effect, so should be used in 'explain' questions but not in 'describe' questions.

Now try this!

1. Describe **one** method used by regions affected by tropical cyclones to prepare for this hazard.

[2 marks]

_____

_____

_____

_____

➡

2. Explain **one** way in which a region affected by tropical cyclones can prepare for this hazard.

[2 marks]

_____

_____

_____

_____

💡 **Tip**   Did you spot the command word? Check that you have **described** for question 1, and **explained** by giving reasons for question 2.

3. Using **Figure 1**, describe one way in which trees adapt to the tropical rainforest.

[2 marks]

Figure 1

_____

_____

_____

_____

_____

4. Explain **one** way in which trees adapt to the tropical rainforest environment.

[2 marks]

_____

_____

_____

_____

💡 **Tip**   Check that you have **described** for question 3, and **explained** by giving reasons for question 4.

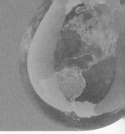

On your marks

Tackling the 3-mark questions

Chains of reasoning

Sometimes, examiners want a little bit more from you than just a single developed answer. This is often the case when there is quite a detailed process involved, or a more complicated explanation. In these cases, examiners set a 3-mark question. The examiners are expecting you to give a 'chain of reasoning' – a sequence of statements, one following on from the other.

What are the common mistakes?

Candidates generally average only 1 mark on 3-mark questions. As with 2-mark questions, the mistake of saying just one thing without any development is common.

Worked example

Explain **one** way in which ecosystems such as rainforests can be protected.

[3 marks]

With 3-mark questions, it is not enough to just name one way in which ecosystems can be protected. To earn 3 marks, you must extend the point (i.e. explain in more detail) twice, as in this example:

Ecosystems such as rainforests can be protected by making it illegal to carry out logging ✓ *so that forest habitats are protected for animals* ✓ *which maintains the biodiversity of the forest.* ✓

> **Tip** 3-mark questions always have six answer lines – a good indication of how much you should write!

Worked example

Explain **one** way in which volcanoes can form along constructive plate margins.

A   **[3 marks]**

As the plates pull apart, a plume of magma rises ✓ *to the surface to fill the gap. At constructive plate* B *margins this is often* basaltic lava which flows easily away from the margin ✓ *before solidifying. As more lava rises* another layer of rock is formed on top of the first to form a shield volcano. ✓

C

> **Tip** When you're explaining how one thing leads to another, you should use **connectives**. These are words linking sentences or phrases together. They include:
>
> - 'because'
> - 'therefore'
> - 'so that'
> - 'which leads to'
> - 'which means that'
>
> See how many you can use in the answers to the questions on the next page!

Examiner feedback

This candidate makes three separate statements, which are highlighted and marked **A**, **B** and **C**.

This is a good example of a 'chain of reasoning'. Notice how the sentences form a sequence or chain – **A** happens, followed by **B**, followed by **C**. The sequence is:

A the rising plume of magma (1 mark)

B the basaltic lava flowing away from the margin (1 mark)

C the layers building up to form a volcano (1 mark).

So this candidate gets 3 marks.

Now try this!

1. Explain **one** difference between the type of volcanoes found at constructive plate boundaries and those found at destructive plate boundaries.

[3 marks]

_____

_____

_____

_____

_____

_____

2. Explain how **one** change in land use can increase the risk of river flooding.

[3 marks]

_____

_____

_____

_____

_____

_____

3. Explain **one** impact of economic development on the rate of urbanisation in a low-income country (LIC) or newly emerging economy (NEE).

[3 marks]

_____

_____

_____

_____

_____

_____

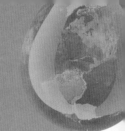

On your marks

Managing the statistics questions

Tackling statistical questions

Ten per cent of all marks in GCSE Geography are for maths and statistical skills. Data are essential to Geography, so you need to be able to handle data and make some fairly straightforward calculations.

This section will give you practice at calculating:

- percentages
- measures of central tendency (a value that represents the centre of a set of data), usually known as mean, median and mode.

Remember, you're allowed to use a calculator in a Geography exam. That will help you, but you do need to show your workings for many questions.

What are the common mistakes?

Candidates often make the following mistakes in exam questions:

- When calculating percentages, candidates often get the data the wrong way round, especially when trying to calculate changes over a period of time.
- They often mix up mean, median and mode.

💡 **Tip**

- For 1-mark questions, you don't need to show any working. It's the answer that will get you a mark.
- For 2-mark questions, you get 1 mark for the answer, and the second mark for showing your working. So never just work out the answer on a calculator – you'll lose out on a mark!

Worked example

Study **Figure 1** below. It shows mean monthly temperatures in a city in southern England.

Figure 1

	Jan	Feb	Mar	Apr	May	Jun	Jul	Aug	Sep	Oct	Nov	Dec
Mean monthly temp. (°C)	5	5	7	10	13	15	18	17	15	10	7	5

Calculate the modal value of the mean monthly temperature shown in **Figure 1**.

[1 mark]

Two candidates gave their answers as follows.

Answer 1: _____ 5 _____

This answer is correct. The modal value means the number that occurs most. In **Figure 1**, the most commonly occurring number is 5.

Answer 2: _____ 10.58 _____

This answer is wrong. Look back at **Figure 1** and you might work out where the candidate made a mistake. This answer is the mean temperature, not the modal value. So the candidate clearly confused the two terms.

💡 **Tip**

Mean = Add up all the values and then divide by the number of values

Median = The middle value in a ranked data set

Mode = The most common value

Now try this!

1. **Figure 1** shows climate data for central Mali.

Figure 1

	Jan	Feb	Mar	Apr	May	Jun	Jul	Aug	Sep	Oct	Nov	Dec
Temp. (°C)	21.2	24	27.4	30.7	33	33.2	31.8	30.3	30.3	29.4	25.8	21.9
Rainfall (mm)	0.1	0.6	1.6	6.3	16.5	40.8	83.5	114.2	64	16.3	1.3	0.2

➡ Calculate the following:

1.1. The mean annual temperature.

[1 mark]

_____

1.2. The annual range in temperature.

[1 mark]

_____

1.3. The annual total rainfall.

[1 mark]

_____

1.4. The percentage of rain that falls during the rainy season of June–September inclusive. Answer to one decimal place.

[3 marks]

Show your working.

Percentage of rain =   %

2.   Study **Figure 2**. It shows changes in economic data for India between 1991 and 2019.

Figure 2

	India 1991	India 2019
GDP total (US$) in PPP	1.2 trillion	9 trillion
GDP per capita (US$) in PPP	1150	6700
Exports value (US$)	17.2 billion	572 billion
Imports value (US$)	24.7 billion	624 billion

2.1. By how many times did India's GDP increase between 1991 and 2019?

[1 mark]

_____

2.2. Calculate the value of the difference between exports and imports in 2019.

[1 mark]

_____

Manipulating statistics

Exam questions that ask you to manipulate data are common in GCSE Geography. This means processing the data and going beyond making a few calculations such as means or percentages.

These questions are harder because you have to think about the data and know some specialist terms. You could be asked to work with:

- quartiles and inter-quartile ranges
- percentiles
- two sets of data, usually to see whether there's a relationship
- data to make predictions and calculations based on trends (known as extrapolation).

What are the common mistakes?

A surprising number of students get no marks in more complex statistical exam questions. Percentiles, quartiles and inter-quartile ranges are only taught in higher-tier Maths, so you may have studied these for the first time in your GCSE Geography course.

Make sure you understand the terminology at least. Statistical skills are included in the *GCSE 9-1 Geography AQA Student Book*:

- Quartiles and inter-quartile ranges can be found on page 375.
- Using percentiles is on page 376.
- Dealing with two data sets is on pages 370 and 377, and trend lines on page 377.
- Extrapolation is on page 377.

Worked example

1. A group of students carried out some fieldwork to test the relationship between soil depth and plant height. **Figure 1** shows their results.

Figure 1

Site number	Soil depth (cm)	Plant height (cm)
1	0.0	4.0
2	3.2	1.5
3	3.6	6.0
4	1.9	11.5
5	10.1	22.0
6	15.2	65.0
7	20.2	92.0
8	23.8	103.0
9	32.0	129.0
10	32.0	187.4

1.1. Name **one** type of graph that the students could use to see whether there is a relationship between soil depth and plant height.

[1 mark]

A scattergraph ✓

1.2. Explain how you would draw this graph.

[3 marks]

I would draw two axes ✓, one for soil depth and the other for plant height ✓, so that I could then plot the points for each of the ten places. ✓

Examiner feedback

The candidate's answer to 1.1 is correct because a scattergraph is used to find a relationship between two sets of data. (If the candidate had answered 'bar graph' then this would be incorrect because bar graphs are used to show single variables, e.g. the number of cars that passed by in a traffic count.)

For 1.2 the candidate also gets full marks for explaining all three stages in drawing a scattergraph.

Now try this!

1. Students took 16 samples of river sediment at different points downstream.

   Study **Figure 1**, a dispersion graph, which plots their data.

   Tip Remember that 'quartile' means 'divided into four'. Here, for example, the top 4 samples are called the 'upper quartile' and the lower 4 samples are the 'lower quartile'.

   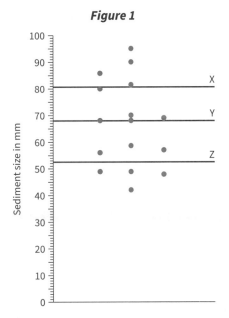

   Figure 1

   1.1. On the graph, three values are labelled X, Y and Z.
   Complete the table below by writing the correct letter against each term.

   [2 marks]

Value	Letter
Median	
Lower quartile	
Upper quartile	

   1.2. Identify **two** values on **Figure 1** which could be the modal value.

   [2 marks]

   _____ and _____

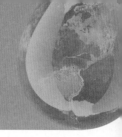

On your marks
Excelling at 4-mark questions

4-mark questions using a resource

In this section you'll learn how to maximise marks on 4-mark questions that use a resource, such as a photo or table of data. 4-mark questions:

- involve writing short paragraphs. To succeed with questions worth 4 or more marks, you must write in full sentences.

- are marked using levels (see page 9). The examiner reads your whole answer first and then decides what mark to give it using specific criteria.

What are the common mistakes?

Like the question below, many 4-mark questions begin with the words 'Using **Figure 1** and your own understanding…'. Many candidates use one or the other – but not both! If you only use **either** Figure 1 **or** your own understanding, you can only gain Level 1 in the mark scheme. That means a maximum of 2 marks. To give you the best chance of receiving high marks, make sure you mention features from Figure 1 **as well as** your own knowledge. First, look at the question below.

Questions using 'suggest'

Study **Figure 1**. It shows a house damaged by Typhoon Haiyan in 2013.

Figure 1

Using **Figure 1** and your own understanding, suggest **two** reasons why tropical storms have such a big impact in low-income countries (LICs).

[4 marks]

> **For this 4-mark 'suggest' question, you will:**
>
> 1. Plan your answer
>
> 2. Mark an answer
>
> 3. Mark a different answer

> 💡 **Tip** Always 'spot the geography' in the question first – it may help to settle you into thinking about the question. In this example it's 'tropical storms'.

1. Plan your answer

Before attempting to answer the question, remember to **BUG** it. That means:

✓ **Box** the command word, as shown below.

✓ **Underline** the following:

- The focus of the question

- The evidence you need to answer the question

- The number of reasons you need to give for 4 marks.

✓ **Glance** back over the question to make sure you included everything in your answer.

Worked example

Use 'BUGs' like this one to plan your own answers.

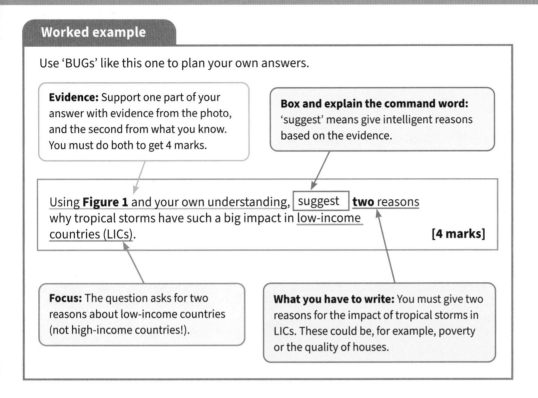

Evidence: Support one part of your answer with evidence from the photo, and the second from what you know. You must do both to get 4 marks.

Box and explain the command word: 'suggest' means give intelligent reasons based on the evidence.

Using **Figure 1** and your own understanding, suggest **two** reasons why tropical storms have such a big impact in low-income countries (LICs). **[4 marks]**

Focus: The question asks for two reasons about low-income countries (not high-income countries!).

What you have to write: You must give two reasons for the impact of tropical storms in LICs. These could be, for example, poverty or the quality of houses.

Use the **PEEL** technique (**P**oint, **E**vidence, **E**xplanation, **L**ink) to help you draft your answer. You will have many opportunities to practise PEEL throughout this chapter. PEEL will help you in your GCSE exam to write answers in the clearest way.

Activity 1

Answer the questions below (which are based on the exam question above). They demonstrate the first three stages of PEEL.

(a) **Point:** Make **two** points (i.e. two reasons) why tropical storms have such a big impact on developing countries.

- _____

- _____

(b) **Evidence:** Include **one** piece of evidence from the photo and **one** from your own knowledge to support the above points.

- _____

- _____

(c) **Explanation:** Give **one** reason for each point.

- _____

- _____

(You don't need to use the 'Link' technique for 4-mark questions. But you'll learn more about how to use 'Link' when you're answering 6- and 9-mark questions on pages 72–91).

> **Tip** Aim for quality not quantity! 4-mark answers are not only based on the number of points you make, but also on the overall quality of your answer. This means including content from the figure and your own knowledge, and giving good reasons.

2. Mark this answer

Read through the sample answer below and decide whether it's a good answer or not. Do this by following these steps.

(a) Pick out whether it includes any good points, evidence and explanations. Highlight or underline any:

- points in red
- evidence in blue
- explanations in orange.

Question recap

Using **Figure 1** and your own understanding, suggest **two** reasons why tropical storms have such a big impact in low-income countries (LICs).

The photo shows a wooden building which has fallen down, probably during the high winds in a tropical storm which will have destroyed it. The people who live there are probably poor and have no resistance to storms like this.

In the photo, the different building materials (bits of wood, bamboo) show the building was probably cheap to build, but weak. This is typical of developing countries where many people might be very poor.

(b) Use the mark scheme below (just like examiners do) to decide what mark to give. 4-mark questions are not marked using individual points, but by choosing a level and a mark based on the quality of the answer as a whole.

Level	Marks	Descriptor	Examples
2 (Clear)	3–4	• Shows accurate understanding of impacts by applying relevant knowledge and understanding to the photo. • Makes clear and effective use of the photo to explain the impacts of a tropical storm.	• *'Many buildings in developing countries are weak and would collapse during a strong tropical storm. This is because they have few building regulations.'* • *'The photo shows poor-quality housing built from wood, which could not stand up to the high winds in a tropical storm.'*
1 (Basic)	1–2	• Shows some limited understanding of impacts by applying some knowledge and understanding to the photo. • Makes limited use of the photo to explain the impacts of a tropical storm.	• *'Houses in many poorer countries are built from cheap materials which would fall down in a storm.'* • *'Many people living in developing countries do not have money to build houses with proper materials.'*
	0	No relevant content.	

(c) Fill in the marking table below showing the strengths and weaknesses of the answer.

Strengths of this answer	
Ways to improve this answer	
The level I would give this answer is…	**The mark I would give this answer is…**

Worked example

The sample answer in Activity 2 is marked below. The text has been coloured to show the strengths of the answer, showing:

- points in red

- evidence in blue

- explanations in orange.

Evidence: wooden buildings visible in the photo

Point: the building has fallen down, an essential part of the answer

Explanation: suggests that high winds have destroyed this building and makes the link to tropical storms

The photo shows a wooden building which has fallen down, probably during the high winds in a tropical storm which will have destroyed it. The people who live there are probably poor and have no resistance to storms like this.

Explanation: suggests people are poor with no resistance to tropical storms

In the photo, the different building materials (bits of wood, bamboo) show the building was probably cheap to build, but weak. This is typical of developing countries where many people might be very poor.

Evidence: specific building materials from the photo

Point: the building was cheap to build, which links to the previous point

Examiner feedback

This is a good example of a top Level 2 answer.

- The answer explains the link between the high winds in a tropical storm and the quality of the building. This shows that the candidate has used evidence in the photo.

- The answer explains the weather conditions found during a tropical storm, and how this might affect houses built from cheap, weak building materials. This shows the candidate's understanding.

- In both parts of the answer, the candidate refers directly to the photo.

By meeting the descriptors for Level 2 fully, the answer earns all 4 marks.

3. Mark a different answer

 **Activity 3**

Now you've marked an answer with some guidance, try marking this different answer to the question on page 56.

- Use the mark scheme and highlight the answer like you did before, using the same colours.

- The mark that the answer got from the examiner is in the answers section at the back of this book.

Wooden shacks like the one in the photo would not be able to stand up to strong hurricane winds so they would fall down.

People in poor countries often live in houses like this on land that isn't theirs.

Questions using 'explain'

Now use the BUG and PEEL stages from pages 56–57 to tackle a different 4-mark question.

Figure 1 shows three measures of development for three countries.

Figure 1

Country	HDI	Death rate per 1000 population	Percentage of population with access to safe water
Japan	0.891	9.51	100
Brazil	0.755	6.58	98
Zimbabwe	0.509	10.13	77

Explain the strengths and limitations of any **one** of the indicators in **Figure 1** in seeking to understand a country's level of development.

[4 marks]

> For this 4-mark 'explain' question, you will:
>
> 1. Plan your answer
>
> 2. Write your answer
>
> 3. Mark your answer
>
> 4. Mark a different answer
>
> 5. Improve an answer

1. Plan your answer

 **Activity 4**

BUG your answer!

Before attempting to answer the question, remember to **BUG** it. Use the guidelines on page 57 to annotate the question in the boxes below.

Evidence:

Box and explain the command word:

Explain the strengths and limitations of any **one** of the indicators in **Figure 1** in seeking to understand a country's level of development.

[4 marks]

Focus:

What you have to write:

Activity 5

PEEL your answer!

Use the PEEL guidance on page 57 to help you structure your answer.

(a) Point: Make **two** points.

- _____

- _____

(b) Evidence: Include **one** advantage of the chosen indicator and **one** disadvantage.

- _____

- _____

(c) Explanation: Give **one** reason for each point.

- _____

- _____

(You don't need to use the 'Link' technique for 4-mark questions.)

2. Write your answer

Activity 6

Explain the strengths and limitations of any **one** of the indicators in **Figure 1** in seeking to understand a country's level of development.

[4 marks]

_____

_____

_____

_____

_____

_____

_____

_____

Tip For Activity 6, check that you have written about one strength and one limitation.

Excelling at 4-mark questions

3. Mark your answer

 **Activity 7**

(a) To help you to identify if your answer includes well-structured points, highlight the:

- points in red
- explanations in orange
- evidence in blue.

(b) Use the mark scheme below to decide what mark to give your answer.

Remember, 4-mark questions are not marked using individual points. Instead, choose a level and a mark based on the quality of the answer as a whole.

Level	Marks	Descriptor	Examples
2 (Clear)	3–4	• Shows a good understanding of one measure of development, with one clear advantage and one clear disadvantage. • Shows a good understanding of how that measure of development can show a positive or negative picture of a country.	• *'The percentage of people with access to safe water is a useful measure since it shows water quality, which would probably result from higher spending on water.'* • *'Water quality shows a country is developing well because, generally, the higher a country's GNI, the better its water, and in turn this would lead to better health.'*
1 (Basic)	1–2	• Shows limited understanding of one measure of development, and struggles to give advantages and disadvantages. • Shows limited understanding of how that measure of development can show a positive or negative picture of a country.	• *'Death rate data helps to show how good a country is because if people have good health then they don't die.'* • *'Death rates are high in developing countries because living conditions aren't good.'*
	0	No relevant content.	

(c) Fill in the marking table below, showing the strengths and weaknesses of your answer.

Strengths of my answer	
Ways to improve my answer	
The level I would give my answer is…	**The mark I would give my answer is…**

 Tip To reach the top marks in Level 2, you must:

a) show that you know the meaning of the development indicator that you have chosen
b) be able to explain one advantage and one disadvantage of the development indicator.

If you cover only one of these, you won't get beyond Level 1.

4. Mark a different answer

 **Activity 8**

Read through this sample answer to the same question.

(a) Annotate the answer with the three colours used in Activity 7 above.

HDI is a good measure of a country's development, because it shows how well developed a country is socially as well as economically. It is a single figure that combines GDP (to show how wealthy a country is) with literacy (which shows the level of education) and infant mortality (which shows the level of healthcare). So it is a good way of showing how much money is spent on health and education. HDI has a disadvantage because wealthy countries might not have a high HDI figure if wealth is concentrated in the hands of a few wealthy people (like Saudi Arabia), and so does not get spent on most of the population.

(b) Use the mark scheme in Activity 7 to decide how many marks the answer is worth.

(c) Fill in the marking table below, showing the strengths and weaknesses of the answer.

Strengths of the answer			
Ways to improve the answer			
The level I would give the answer is...		**The mark I would give the answer is...**	

> **Question recap**
>
> Explain the strengths and limitations of any **one** of the indicators in **Figure 1** (page 60) in seeking to understand a country's level of development.

5. Improve this answer

 **Activity 9**

One candidate wrote this answer to the same question. It earns 1 mark.
Continue writing so that the answer earns 4 marks.

Death rate can measure some things about a country's development, because if people's health is poor then they will die.

_____

_____

_____

_____

_____

_____

Excelling at 4-mark questions

Now try this!

Figure 1 shows a map of the geology and rock resistance of a part of the Dorset coast in southern England.

Figure 1

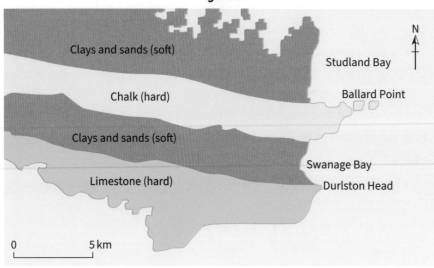

Suggest how geology has influenced coastal landforms along the coast shown in **Figure 1**. Use **Figure 1** and your own understanding.

[4 marks]

> **Tip** Follow each stage in Activities 4 and 5 on pages 60–61 to help you tackle this 4-mark question.

_____

_____

_____

_____

_____

_____

_____

_____

> **Tip** To answer this question fully, check that you know the meanings of these words or phrases:
> - 'geology'
> - 'influenced'
> - 'coastal landforms'.
>   Also, check where you can see coastal landforms on the map.

4-mark questions testing your knowledge & understanding

In this section you'll learn how to maximise marks on 4-mark questions that do not use a resource. They depend on your own knowledge and understanding for a successful answer.

Like other 4-mark questions, they:

- involve short paragraphs of writing
- usually involve explaining a sequence of processes, as the question below shows.

Examiners set this kind of question when they want you to explain how one process leads to another, which leads to another, and so on.

- This kind of explanation is called a 'chain of reasoning'.
- You can learn how to write chains of reasoning by following the steps below.

Worked example

Explain how volcanoes may be formed along constructive plate boundaries.

[4 marks]

To answer this question, you would need to plan a **sequence of statements**. The sequence might look like this:

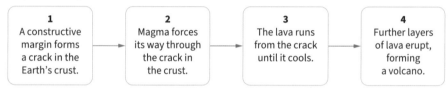

1	2	3	4
A constructive margin forms a crack in the Earth's crust.	Magma forces its way through the crack in the crust.	The lava runs from the crack until it cools.	Further layers of lava erupt, forming a volcano.

The sequence is made up of four statements, written in order. All you need to do is write it out for a perfect 4-mark answer!

Get to know the mark scheme

For the question above, you have to demonstrate:

- knowledge and understanding of a constructive margin
- that you can apply a sequence of processes until you have explained how a volcano forms along a constructive margin.

In the mark scheme below, notice how Level 2 rewards clear understanding of a constructive margin, with a sequence of processes leading to the formation of a volcano.

A Level 1 answer would show some knowledge of the term 'constructive margin', but would not really connect it to the processes leading to a volcano.

Level	Marks	Descriptor	Examples
2 (Clear)	3–4	• Demonstrates a clear understanding of a constructive margin and the processes by which magma reaches the surface. • Application is accurate, with a clear sequence of the processes leading to the formation of a volcano.	• 'A constructive margin forms a crack in the Earth's crust, which magma forces its way through.' • 'The lava runs from the crack until it cools, with later layers of lava forming a volcano.'
1 (Basic)	1–2	• Shows some limited understanding of a constructive margin and the processes by which magma reaches the surface. • Application is weak, with little or no sequencing of the processes leading to the formation of a volcano.	• 'A constructive margin is a crack in the Earth's surface.' • 'Volcanoes form along this crack when hot lava erupts.'
	0	No relevant content.	

Questions using 'explain'

> Explain how **one** hard method of coastal engineering can protect the coastline.
>
> [4 marks]

1. Plan your answer

 **Activity 1**

For two 4-mark 'explain' questions, you will:

1. Plan your answer
2. Mark an answer
3. Answer a different question
4. Mark your answer

(a) Using the flowchart below, write out the chain of four statements needed to answer this question.

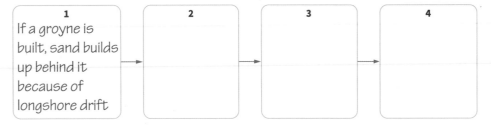

1	2	3	4
If a groyne is built, sand builds up behind it because of longshore drift			

(b) Write four examples in the mark scheme below that you would look for in an answer to this question – 1 and 2 for Level 2; 3 and 4 for Level 1. You could use your chain of reasoning to help you.

Level	Marks	Descriptor	Examples
2 (Clear)	3–4	• Demonstrates a clear understanding of one hard method of coastal engineering and its purpose. • Application is accurate, with a clear sequence of the processes leading to a problem further along the coast.	1 2
1 (Basic)	1–2	• Shows some limited understanding of one hard method of coastal engineering and its purpose. • Application is weak, with little or no sequencing of the processes leading to a problem further along the coast.	3 4
	0	No relevant content.	

2. Mark an answer

 **Activity 2**

Mark this answer using your mark scheme above. Annotate the answer with your own 'Examiner's feedback'.

The job of beach groynes is to trap sand brought by longshore drift. However, by stopping longshore drift, they starve other places of sand further along the coast. Where this happens, there is less beach so the sea can reach the cliff foot and erode it more easily.

3. Answer a different question

 **Activity 3**

Use the steps in Activity 1 on page 66 to help you write your own answer to a different 4-mark question.

> Explain how a change of land use could lead to an increased risk of flooding.
>
> **[4 marks]**

_____

_____

_____

_____

_____

_____

_____

_____

4. Write a mark scheme

Activity 4

(a) Write four examples in the mark scheme that you would look for in an answer to this question.

Level	Marks	Descriptor	Examples
2 (Clear)	3–4	• Demonstrates a clear understanding of how changes of land use can affect rivers and the likelihood of flooding. • Application is accurate with a clear sequence of the processes leading to flooding.	1 2
1 (Basic)	1–2	• Shows some limited understanding of how changes of land use can affect rivers and the likelihood of flooding. • Application is weak with little or no sequencing of the processes leading to flooding.	3 4
	0	No relevant content.	

(b) Mark your answer to Activity 3 using this mark scheme.

Strengths of the answer	
Ways to improve the answer	

The level I would give the answer is...		The mark I would give the answer is...	

Extra practice questions

Now try this!

1. Study **Figure 1**, which shows the location of derelict land and the most deprived areas of Glasgow.

Tip Use the steps in Activity 1 on page 66 to help you answer these questions.

Figure 1

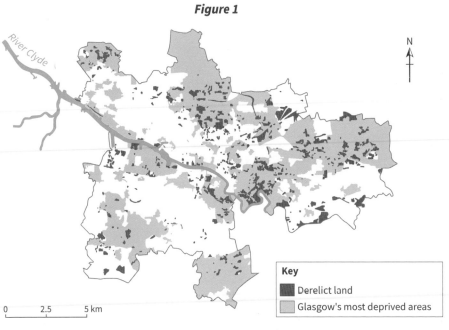

Key

■ Derelict land

▨ Glasgow's most deprived areas

0   2.5   5 km

Using **Figure 1**, suggest reasons why derelict land and the most deprived areas of Glasgow can be found in similar parts of the city.

[4 marks]

_____

_____

_____

_____

_____

_____

_____

_____

2. Study **Figure 2**, showing a slum area in a megacity in one of the world's low-income countries (LICs) or newly emerging economies (NEEs).

Figure 2

Using **Figure 2**, explain how urban growth in low-income countries (LICs) or newly emerging economies (NEEs) has affected quality of life.

[4 marks]

3. Study **Figure 3**, which shows ice coverage in the Arctic in 2012.

Figure 3

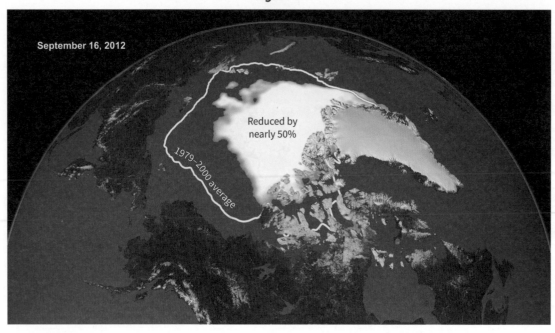

September 16, 2012

Reduced by nearly 50%

1979–2000 average

Using **Figure 3** and your own understanding, outline the evidence for climate change.

[4 marks]

_____

_____

_____

_____

_____

_____

_____

_____

> **Tip** **Figure 3** shows one piece of 'evidence for climate change', which you should describe. In the question, 'your own understanding' means consider other evidence, such as ice cores, rising sea levels and seasonal changes. Your answer should refer to several factors in order to describe the 'big picture'.

 **Activity**

Review your answers to 'Now try this!' questions 1, 2 and 3 on pages 68–70 by completing the marking tables below.

Question 1

Strengths of my answer	
Ways to improve my answer	

The level I would give my answer is…		The mark I would give my answer is…	

Question 2

Strengths of my answer	
Ways to improve my answer	

The level I would give my answer is…		The mark I would give my answer is…	

Question 3

Strengths of my answer	
Ways to improve my answer	

The level I would give my answer is…		The mark I would give my answer is…	

On your marks
Stepping up to 6-mark questions

In this section you'll learn how to tackle 6-mark questions that use 'explain', 'suggest' or 'discuss' as a command word.

6-mark questions differ from 4-mark ones:

- They are marked using three levels, not two.
- Levels 1 and 2 are the same standard as Levels 1 and 2 in the 4-mark questions.
- Level 3 is more challenging, worth 5–6 marks. It means writing to a higher standard.

Explain or suggest – what's the difference?

- With 'explain', you're expected to **know**, as these questions test you on what you've been taught in the specification. You could be asked to explain a statement, for example.
- With 'suggest', examiners accept you might **not know**, but are confident that after being taught Geography at GCSE level you should be able to work it out easily enough.

What are the common mistakes?

- Many 6-mark questions begin 'Using **Figure 1** and your own understanding…'.
- Many candidates use one or the other, but not both!
- If you only use **either** Figure 1 **or** your own understanding, you can only get Level 2 in the mark scheme. That means a maximum of 4 marks.

To succeed, make sure you mention features from the figure **as well as** your own understanding.

Questions using 'explain'

First, look at the question below.

Study **Figure 1**, showing deposition of sediment at Hurst Castle, Hampshire.

Figure 1

Using **Figure 1** and your own understanding, explain how different landforms may be created by the deposition of sediment.

[6 marks]

Tip Don't leave out the 6-mark questions just because they're harder. It's actually quite straightforward to earn 3–4 marks just by explaining what you know.

Tip A 4-mark question might ask:

'Explain two impacts of a volcanic eruption on the climate'.

A 6-mark question might ask:

'"Volcanic eruptions can cause important changes to the global climate."

Using evidence, explain this statement.'

Tip Note that this question is about Coasts. If you have studied River landscapes and Glacial landscapes, work through these pages using a different photo from the *GCSE 9-1 Geography AQA Student Book*:

- For River landscapes, use Photo A on page 134.
- For Glacial landscapes, use Photo C at the top of page 153.

For this 6-mark 'explain' question, you will:

1. **Plan your answer**

2. **Mark an answer**

1. Plan your answer

Before attempting to answer the question, remember to **BUG** it. That means:

✓ **Box** the command word, as shown below.

✓ **Underline** the following:

- The focus of the question
- The evidence you need to answer the question
- The number of reasons you need to give for 6 marks.

✓ **Glance** back over the question to make sure you included everything in your answer.

Worked example

Use 'BUGs' like this one to plan your own answers.

> **Evidence:** Support one part of your answer with evidence from the photo, and the second part from what you know. You must do both to get 6 marks.

> **Box and explain the command word:** 'Explain' means you have to give reasons for what happens.

> **Using Figure 1 and your own understanding,** ⬚explain⬚ how **different landforms** may be created by **deposition** of sediment. **[6 marks]**

> **Focus:** The question asks for landforms created by **deposition**, not erosion!

> **What you have to write:** The question asks for 'different landforms'. For 6 marks, you must write about two in detail, or three in less detail.

Use the **PEEL** technique to help you draft your answer.

 **Activity 1**

Answer the questions below (which are based on the exam question above).

(a) Point: Make **two** points about how **two** different landforms are created by deposition.

- _____

- _____

(b) Evidence: Include **one** piece of evidence from the photo and **one** from your own understanding to support the above points.

- _____

- _____

(c) Explanation: Give **two** reasons that show how the landforms have formed.

- _____

- _____

(d) Link: Round each point off by linking it back to the question (start with a phrase like 'This shows how deposition has…'). It helps you to stay with the question.

- _____

- _____

> 💡 **Tip** Make sure you explain! Don't just describe. If the question asks you to explain, it wants you to give **reasons** why something happens. For example, 'Explain how a named landform is caused by erosion' would want you to say **how** erosion processes led to its formation, not simply give a description of the landform.

2. Mark this answer

Activity 2

Read through the sample answer below and decide how well the student has answered the question. Do this by following these steps.

(a) Pick out whether it includes any good points, evidence and explanations. Highlight or underline the text to show the following strengths of the answer:

- Points in red
- Evidence in blue
- Explanations in orange
- <u>Links back to the question</u> underlined

The photo shows a spit that has been formed from sand washed up by the waves on the beach. The waves approach at an angle and the swash takes the sand up the beach, then it runs back down in a zig-zag pattern. Then another wave picks it up, and deposits it further along the beach, and so on, until it forms an extension of land as shown in the photo. The sand moves along the beach until it reaches a river, and the photo shows how the river current has shaped it where the water runs out to sea. It looks like the river in the photo has shaped the spit into a hook as it has grown.

Another landform formed by deposition is a sand bar, which is just like a spit except that there is no river to stop the movement of sand. The sand keeps on moving until it cuts off a lake or lagoon. So this shows how important deposition is to forming this landform.

> **Question recap**
>
> Using **Figure 1** and your own understanding, explain how different landforms may be created by the deposition of sediment.

(b) Use the mark scheme below to decide what mark to give. 6-mark questions are not marked using individual points, but by choosing a level and a mark based on the quality of the answer as a whole.

Level	Marks	Descriptor	Examples
3 (Detailed)	5–6	• Shows thorough application of knowledge and understanding to analyse information, giving detailed explanation of the formation of coastal features. • Makes full analysis of the photo, using evidence to support the answer.	• 'The coastal spit shown has been formed by two sets of processes. The main one is longshore drift, caused by winds creating waves that hit the shore at an angle and deposit sand.' • 'Figure 1 shows a coastal spit that has forced the river to divert from where it used to reach the sea.'
2 (Clear)	3–4	• Demonstrates specific and accurate knowledge of coastal processes and landforms. • Shows thorough understanding of the links between coastal processes and landforms.	• 'Coastal spits are formed when waves break on the shore at an angle and take sediment along the coast, forming a long sandy headland into the water.' • 'Figure 1 shows how the river stops the spit from forming a bar, which would join the two bits of coast together.'
1 (Basic)	1–2	• Demonstrates some knowledge of coastal processes and landforms. • Shows limited geographical understanding of the links between coastal processes and landforms.	• 'The spit comes from waves that break on the beach and longshore drift takes place.' • 'The photo shows a long sandy beach that has been deposited by waves.'
	0	No relevant content.	

(c) Fill in the marking table below showing the strengths and weaknesses of the answer.

Strengths of this answer		
Ways to improve this answer		
The level I would give this answer is...		**The mark I would give this answer is...**

Worked example

The sample answer in Activity 2 is marked below, so you can compare your marking with this. The text has been coloured and underlined to show the following strengths of the answer:

- Points in red

- Evidence in blue

- Explanations in orange

- Links back to the question underlined

Point: the candidate names a correct landform and states that it's formed of sand

Explanation: the process of how the spit begins to form is described

Evidence: the candidate supports the process with evidence from the photo. This kind of evidence is important when you need to explain processes as a sequence of stages.

The photo shows a spit that has been formed from sand washed up by the waves on the beach. The waves approach at an angle and the swash takes the sand up the beach, then it runs back down in a zig-zag pattern. Then another wave picks it up, and deposits it further along the beach, and so on, until it forms an extension of land as shown in the photo. The sand moves along the beach until it reaches a river, and the photo shows how the river current has shaped it where the water runs out to sea. It looks like the river in the photo has shaped the spit into a hook as it has grown.

Evidence: the photo supports the part in the process played by the river

Evidence: the photo supports how the river is affected by the spit

Another landform formed by deposition is a sand bar, which is just like a spit except that there is no river to stop the movement of sand. The sand keeps on moving until it cuts off a lake or lagoon. So this shows how important deposition is to forming this landform.

Point: the candidate names a second depositional landform

Explanation: the process of bar formation is explained

Link: this is where the candidate links back to the original question

Examiner feedback

This candidate reaches Level 3 – but only just! The key is in the question, which asks for **different** landforms to be explained. This candidate spends most of the time explaining the spit, and has less time in which to explain a second landform. It would be better to split the time equally between the two landforms to reach Level 3.

That said, this answer is Level 3.

- It describes landform formation in some detail. Landforms are named accurately.

- It explains the formation in some detail as a sequence of events. The difference between a spit and a bar is explained.

- It refers to the photo well, by recognising and naming the landform, and explaining the impact of the spit on the route taken by the river.

By explaining one landform fully, and the second one partly, the answer is a low Level 3 in quality, so it's worth 5 marks.

Questions using 'suggest'

This time, the command word is 'suggest'. This means that you should look at **Figure 1** and think about what you know about rainforest clearance. Then make suggestions about what could happen based on **Figure 1** and what you know and understand.

Study **Figure 1**. It shows a rainforest in Borneo, Indonesia that has been cleared to make way for a plantation for farming.

Figure 1

Using **Figure 1** and your own understanding, suggest the impacts of rainforest clearance in Indonesia.

[6 marks]

For this 6-mark 'suggest' question, you will:

1. Plan your answer

2. Write your answer

3. Mark your answer

4. Mark a different answer

1. Plan your answer

 **Activity 1**

Before attempting to answer the question, remember to **BUG** it. There are some hints about what to write in the boxes on page 73, and you should use these to annotate the boxes below.

Evidence:	Box and explain the command word:

Using **Figure 1** and your own understanding, suggest the impacts of rainforest clearance in Indonesia.

[6 marks]

Focus:	What you have to write:

 **Activity 2**

Use the **PEEL** guidance on page 73 to help you structure your answer.

(a) Point:

- _____

- _____

(b) Evidence:

- _____

- _____

(c) Explanation:

- _____

- _____

(d) Link:

- _____

- _____

2. Write your answer

 **Activity 3**

Using **Figure 1** and your own understanding, suggest the impacts of
rainforest clearance in Indonesia. **[6 marks]**

_____

_____

_____

_____

_____

_____

_____

_____

_____

_____

_____

_____

3. Mark your answer

Activity 4

(a) To help you to identify the strengths of your answer, highlight the:

- points in red

- explanations in orange

- evidence in blue

- and <u>underline</u> any links back to the question.

(b) Use the mark scheme below to decide what mark to give your answer. Remember, 6-mark questions are not marked using individual points. Instead, choose a level and a mark based on the quality of the answer as a whole.

Level	Marks	Descriptor	Examples
3 (Detailed)	5–6	• Provides a range of reasons and impacts that are well developed. There is detailed understanding of these impacts. • Shows thorough identification of the evidence for the impacts of forest clearance in the photo, and understands potential impacts.	• *'The removal of forest cover would expose the soils to heavy tropical rains, which would erode the soil, making the land useless for farming.'* • *'The bare soil in the photo shows how exposed it would be to wind or rain, or tropical sun.'*
2 (Clear)	3–4	• Gives one to two reasons with some development of points. There is a generally accurate understanding of the impacts. • Makes clear and effective use of the photo to explain the impacts of clearing the forest.	• *'Removing the trees would mean less protection for the soil from heavy rain – runoff would occur and probably take the soil with it.'* • *'The photo shows little vegetation to protect the soil so it would probably be lost.'*
1 (Basic)	1–2	• Shows some limited understanding of the impacts by applying some knowledge and understanding to the photo. • Makes limited use of the photo to explain the impacts of clearing the forest.	• *'The land is all bare and there are no trees there. The rain would wash it away.'* • *'The photo shows all the trees have been cut and burned and there's nothing there.'*
	0	No relevant content.	

(c) Fill in the marking table below, showing the strengths and weaknesses of your answer.

Strengths of my answer	
Ways to improve my answer	

The level I would give my answer is…		**The mark I would give my answer is…**	

4. Mark a different answer

 **Activity 5**

Read through the sample answer below. This answers the same question.

(a) Annotate the answer using the three colours and underlining as explained in Activity 4.

> The forest looks like it has been cleared by burning. The land looks full of tree roots, meaning that it will not be easy to plant crops. The soil is black, which is probably ash from all the burnt trees after the fires have gone out. The next time it rains, the ash will probably get washed away because it looks like the land is sloping a bit, and farmers might find there is no soil left by the time they get to plant their crops. There is no wildlife, which probably got killed in the fires. Lots of rainforests get cleared by burning like this.

(b) Use the mark scheme in Activity 4 to decide how many marks the answer is worth.

(c) Fill in the marking table below, showing the strengths and weaknesses of the answer.

> **Question recap**
>
> Using **Figure 1** and your own understanding, suggest the impacts of rainforest clearance in Indonesia.

Strengths of the answer	
Ways to improve the answer	

The level I would give the answer is...		The mark I would give the answer is...	

Hitting Level 3

To get to Level 3, you must:

- explain or suggest two or three reasons or impacts
- give reasons that are developed or well developed
- show detailed understanding, e.g. using terminology such as 'erosion' instead of writing 'the soil gets washed away'
- give evidence for what you see from a photo or other resource given with the question
- give reasons for what you see that show your understanding.

Now try this!

Study **Figure 2**, which shows push and pull factors in the growth of megacities

Figure 2

'The growth of large megacities in LICs or NEEs has brought advantages to the millions of migrants who move to such cities each year.'

Using **Figure 2**, suggest why some might disagree with this statement.

[6 marks]

_____

_____

_____

_____

_____

_____

_____

_____

_____

_____

_____

_____

The level I would give my answer is...		The mark I would give my answer is...	
Comments			

Questions using 'discuss'

This time, the command word is 'discuss'. This means you should look at **Figure 1** and think about what you know about the impacts of international migration on a major UK city that you have studied. Then make suggestions about the impacts based on **Figure 1** and what you know and understand.

Study **Figure 1**. It shows the distribution of Asian-Indian British people in London, 2011.

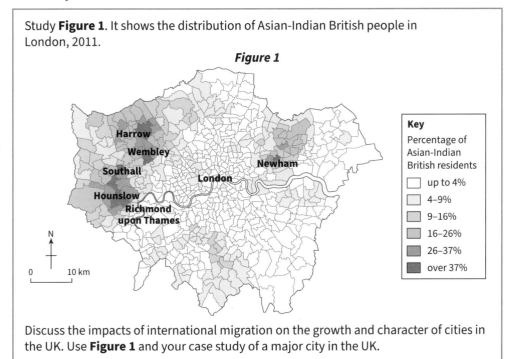

Figure 1

Discuss the impacts of international migration on the growth and character of cities in the UK. Use **Figure 1** and your case study of a major city in the UK.

[6 marks]

> **Tip** 'Discuss' means using a range of examples. Don't just describe and explain! For example, the question 'Discuss the impacts of rainforest clearance' wants you to say whether impacts are positive or negative, or perhaps whether they are economic, social or environmental.

> **For this 6-mark 'discuss' question, you will:**
>
> 1. **Plan your answer**
>
> 2. **Write your answer**
>
> 3. **Mark your answer**
>
> 4. **Mark a different answer**

1. Plan your answer

 **Activity 1**

Before attempting to answer the question, remember to **BUG** it. There are some hints about what to write in the boxes on page 73, and you should use these to annotate the boxes below.

Evidence:	Box and explain the command word:

Discuss the impacts of international migration on the growth and character of cities in the UK. Use **Figure 1** and your case study of a major city in the UK.

[6 marks]

Focus:	What you have to write:

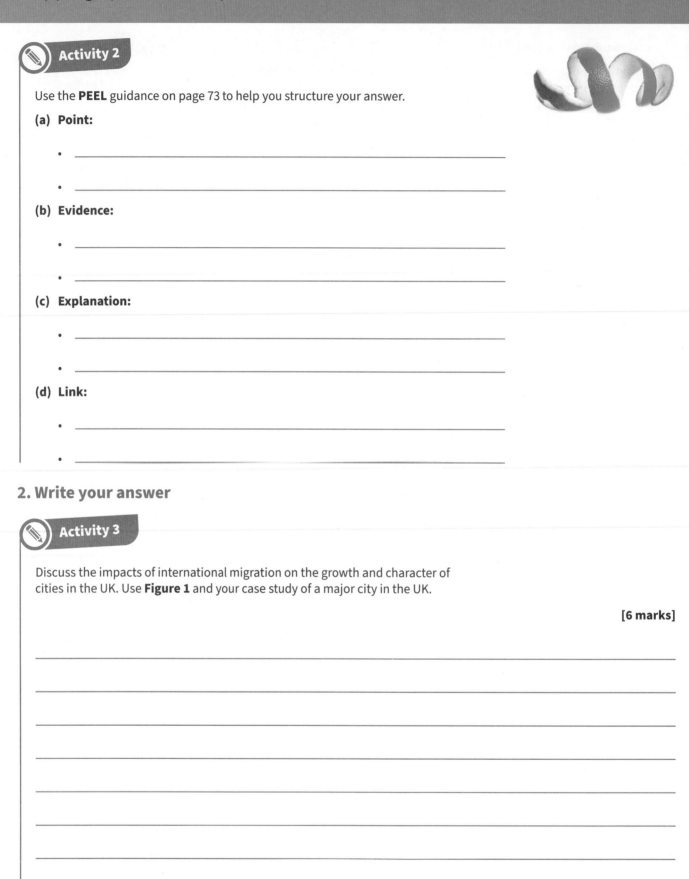

Activity 2

Use the **PEEL** guidance on page 73 to help you structure your answer.

(a) Point:

- _____

- _____

(b) Evidence:

- _____

- _____

(c) Explanation:

- _____

- _____

(d) Link:

- _____

- _____

2. Write your answer

Activity 3

Discuss the impacts of international migration on the growth and character of cities in the UK. Use **Figure 1** and your case study of a major city in the UK.

[6 marks]

_____

_____

_____

_____

_____

_____

_____

_____

_____

_____

_____

_____

3. Mark your answer

 **Activity 4**

(a) To help you to identify the strengths of your answer, highlight the:

- points in red
- explanations in orange
- evidence in blue
- and <u>underline</u> any links back to the question.

(b) Use the mark scheme below to decide what mark to give your answer. Remember, 6-mark questions are not marked using individual points. Instead, choose a level and a mark based on the quality of the answer as a whole.

Level	Marks	Descriptor	Examples
3 (Detailed)	5–6	• Shows thorough understanding of the impacts of international migration on the growth and character of a named UK city. • Shows thorough application of knowledge and understanding in interpreting the map about the impacts of international migration.	• *'The impacts of immigration have been great, especially on the culture of UK cities. In Manchester, the Curry Mile attracts tourists as well as increasing the range of foods in the city.'* • *'Figure 1 shows that immigrants from particular countries, religions or cultures tend to live in areas close to each other, creating suburbs like Southall in west London.'*
2 (Clear)	3–4	• Shows sound understanding of the impacts of international migration on the growth and character of a named UK city. • Shows sound application of knowledge and understanding in interpreting the map about the impacts of international migration.	• *'Immigration has been the reason for half the recent growth of cities such as Bristol. In Bristol there are over 50 languages spoken in the city now.'* • *'Figure 1 shows that immigrants often settle in suburbs where there are cultural or ethnic groups like their own.'*
1 (Basic)	1–2	• Shows limited understanding of the impacts of international migration on the growth and character of a named UK city. • Shows limited application of knowledge and understanding in interpreting the map about the impacts of international migration.	• *'Bristol has a lot of immigrants living there so the city is growing.'* • *'Immigrants often live in the same sorts of areas where they have shops and places of worship they are familiar with and they like living there.'*
	0	No relevant content.	

(c) Fill in the marking table below, showing the strengths and weaknesses of your answer.

Strengths of my answer	
Ways to improve my answer	

The level I would give my answer is…		**The mark I would give my answer is…**	

4. Mark a different answer

 **Activity 5**

Read through the sample answer below. This answers the same question.

(a) Annotate the answer using the three colours and underlining as explained in Activity 4.

> Half of Bristol's population growth in recent years has been due to migrants from overseas, from countries such as Poland, because of the jobs available there such as in construction and the NHS. International migration has affected Bristol because people from over 50 countries have settled there. Over 6000 people live in Bristol who were born in Poland.
>
> Like the map in Figure 1, many immigrants have changed the character of the parts of the city where they live by introducing new shops or places of worship. This changes the culture in cities and there are festivals like the Notting Hill Carnival in London. So immigration has had a big effect on cities.

(b) Use the mark scheme in Activity 4 to decide how many marks the answer is worth.

(c) Fill in the marking table below, showing the strengths and weaknesses of the answer.

<table>
<tr><td>Strengths of the answer</td><td></td><td></td><td></td></tr>
<tr><td>Ways to improve the answer</td><td></td><td></td><td></td></tr>
<tr><td>The level I would give the answer is…</td><td></td><td>The mark I would give the answer is…</td><td></td></tr>
</table>

> **Question recap**
>
> Discuss the impacts of international migration on the growth and character of cities in the UK. Use **Figure 1** (page 81) and your case study of a major city in the UK.

Level 3 checklist

1 Has it included detail?   Yes ☐   No ☐   Partly ☐

Explain what other detail might have been included.

_____

2 Has it explained the impacts of international migration clearly?   Yes ☐   No ☐   Partly ☐

Explain what other detail might have been included.

_____

3 Is there a clear answer to the question?   Yes ☐   No ☐   Partly ☐

Explain what other detail might have been included.

_____

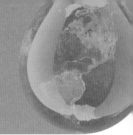

On your marks
Hitting the heights on 9-mark questions

In this section you'll learn how to tackle 9-mark questions that use 'evaluate' and 'do you agree' as the command words.

9-mark questions differ from 6-mark questions:

- 9 marks are available, not 6 – so you must write more.

- The three levels in the mark scheme are geared to a higher standard. This is reflected in the marks: Level 1 ranges from 1 to 3 marks, Level 2 from 4 to 6 marks, and Level 3 from 7 to 9 marks.

- Command words are more demanding. Nine-mark questions use some of the same command words as 6-mark ones (e.g. 'discuss'), but they also use 'evaluate'.

- Like 6-mark questions, you could be given a statement and asked to explain it – but 9-mark questions will also ask you to decide whether you agree or disagree with it. That means you have to develop an argument to support or reject the statement.

What does 'evaluate' mean?

Examiners may use 'evaluate' instead of 'explain' as the command word for 9-mark questions. Here's the key difference:

- With 'explain', you're expected to **know**, as these questions test you on what you've been taught in the specification.

- With 'evaluate', examiners are asking you to **weigh up** different opinions. For example, you could use Typhoon Haiyan as an example to show how the most vulnerable people are affected most by tropical storms. But you could also use Hurricane Sandy as an example to show how the USA has also been affected by tropical storms.

- Remember, 'evaluate' is all about **weighing up evidence and making a judgement** – do you agree or not?

Don't forget SPaG

One of the 9-mark questions on each of Papers 1 and 2 will assess your accuracy of spelling, punctuation, grammar and the use of specialist terminology (SPaG, although as it also includes geographical terminology maybe it should be SPaGT!). You can be awarded up to 3 marks for SPaG for these questions.

What are the common mistakes?

Questions that use 'evaluate' as a command word are setting you up for an argument. To reach top marks, you need to:

- Show your knowledge and understanding that supports the argument. Use phrases such as 'I agree with the statement because…' or 'Evidence that supports the statement includes…'.

- Show your knowledge and understanding of the other side of the argument. Use phrases such as 'On the other hand…' or 'However…'.

- Write a one-sentence conclusion to say whether you think the statement is wrong or right, and why.

> **Tip** Don't ignore the 9-mark questions just because they're tough – have a go! Look for the geography; you can earn 3–4 marks just by explaining what you know, even though you might not be sure how to set up an argument.

> **Tip** Examiners mark SPaG based on:
> - the accuracy of your spelling
> - how well you use paragraphs
> - the accuracy of your punctuation (the use of commas, full stops and semi-colons, etc.).
>
> Try reading your practice answers aloud and see if they leave you gasping for breath – if they do, you need more punctuation!

Questions using 'evaluate'

First, look at the question below.

Study **Figure 1**, which shows estimated increases in global temperatures (°C) 1960–2100.

Figure 1

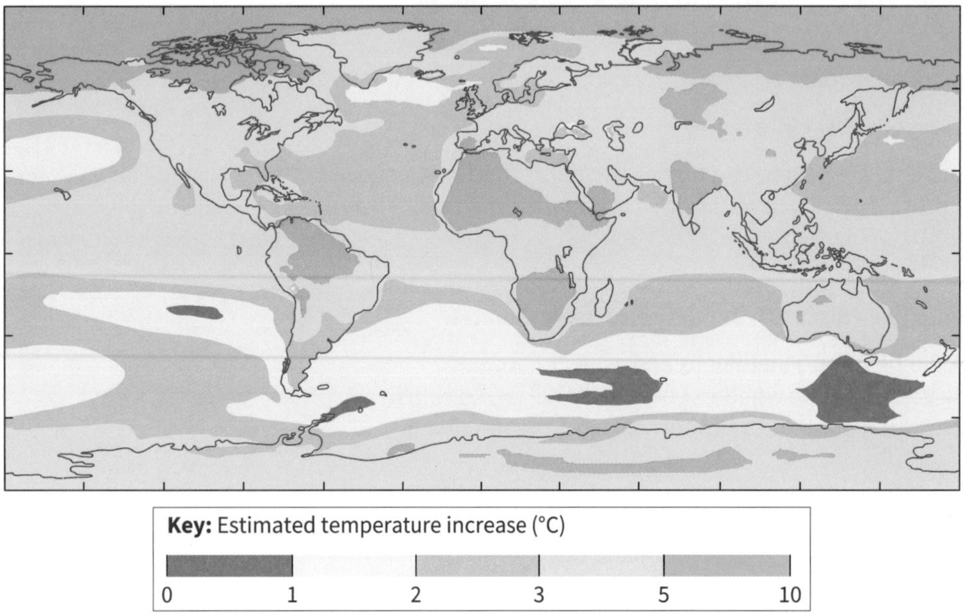

Key: Estimated temperature increase (°C)

| 0 | 1 | 2 | 3 | 5 | 10 |

Using **Figure 1** and your own understanding, evaluate the evidence which suggests that the global climate is currently changing.

[9 marks] [+3 SPaG marks]

> **For this 9-mark 'evaluate' question, you will:**
>
> 1. Plan your answer
>
> 2. Mark an answer

1. Plan your answer

Before attempting to answer the question, remember to **BUG** it. That means:

✓ **Box** the command word, as shown below.

✓ **Underline** the following:

- The focus of the question
- The evidence you need to answer the question
- The number of reasons you need to give for 9 marks.

✓ **Glance** back over the question to make sure you included everything in your answer.

Worked example

Use 'BUGs' like this one to plan your own answers.

> **Box and explain the command word:**
> 'Evaluate' means you need to weigh up both sides of the argument.

> **Evidence:** Support one part of your answer with evidence that global climate is changing, and the second with weighing it up. You must do both to get 9 marks.

Using **Figure 1** and your own understanding, ⟨evaluate⟩ the **evidence** which suggests that the **global climate is currently changing**.

[9 marks] [+3 SPaG marks]

> **Focus:** The question asks for evidence that global climate is changing, **and** you have to weigh it up!

> **What you have to write:** The question asks for evidence of global climate change. For 9 marks, you must write about three points in detail.

Use the **PEEL** technique to help you draft your answer. PEEL will help you in your GCSE exam to write answers in the clearest way.

 **Activity 1**

Answer the questions below (which are based on the exam question above). They demonstrate the four stages of PEEL.

(a) **Point:** Make **three** points about evidence for a changing global climate.

- _____

- _____

- _____

(b) **Evidence:** Include **one** piece of evidence to support each point.

- _____

- _____

- _____

(c) **Explanation:** Weigh up each piece of evidence to show how good it is as evidence for a changing global climate.

- _____

- _____

- _____

(d) **Link:** Link back to the question to show the importance or strength of each piece of evidence. Start with a phrase like 'This evidence strongly supports the argument that the global climate is changing because…'.

- _____

- _____

- _____

> **Tip** 'Evaluate' means deciding how strong each piece of evidence is, showing the strength of the research behind it! Don't just describe and explain. For example, one piece of evidence for a changing global climate might be shrinking glaciers. You need to say whether this is strong evidence or not.

2. Mark this answer

 **Activity 2**

Read through the sample answer on page 88 and decide whether it's a good answer or not. Do this by following these steps.

(a) Pick out whether it includes any good points, evidence and explanations. Highlight or underline the text to show the following strengths of the answer:

- Points in red

- Evidence in blue

- Explanations in orange

- Links back to the question underlined

Globally the climate is warming, with evidence to prove that this is the case. Everywhere in the world is warmer, though seas are warming less than land. This is because greenhouse gas emissions have increased. It is hard to know exactly what temperatures were like in 1900 and more people and organisations record the weather now than at that time, so there were fewer thermometers back then. So some of the evidence could be questionable just because there were fewer recordings previously.

Even if temperature recordings are not completely reliable, there is a lot of evidence to show that sea levels are rising globally by about 20 cm in 100 years, partly because ocean water expands when it warms and so it rises. Many coastal areas are flooding more now, so it is a global process and not just evidence from one place.

Other evidence which shows that temperatures are rising comes from retreating glaciers and ice sheets because they are melting, especially on land areas where there is expected to be an increase of at least 5°C by 2100, as shown in Figure 1. Many glaciers have been photographed for over 100 years, and many in the Alps and on Greenland show that they have retreated a long way from where they were.

> **Question recap**
>
> Using **Figure 1** (page 86) and your own understanding, evaluate the evidence which suggests that the global climate is currently changing.

(b) Use the mark scheme below to decide what mark to give.

Level	Marks	Descriptor	Examples
3 (Detailed)	7–9	• Shows detailed knowledge of the evidence for a changing climate. • Shows thorough geographical understanding of the processes by which the climate may be changing globally. • Shows application of knowledge and understanding in a coherent and reasoned way in evaluating the evidence for climate change.	• 'Figure 1 shows that everywhere in the world is affected by a changing climate to varying degrees.' • 'Sea level is increasing due to rising global temperatures, which melt ice caps, from which more water goes into the sea.' • 'This is likely to be reliable evidence as the IPCC consists of thousands of the world's best scientists.'
2 (Clear)	4–6	• Shows clear knowledge of the evidence for a changing climate. • Shows some geographical understanding of the processes by which the climate may be changing globally. • Shows reasonable application of knowledge and understanding in evaluating the evidence for climate change.	• 'Figure 1 shows that the global climate is changing and getting warmer.' • 'Global sea levels have risen due to global warming, which increases temperatures and melts ice caps and glaciers, which go into the sea.' • 'We know sea levels are rising because countries with coastlines are getting flooded.'
1 (Basic)	1–3	• Shows limited knowledge of the evidence for a changing climate. • Shows slight geographical understanding of the processes by which the climate may be changing globally. • Shows limited application of knowledge and understanding in evaluating the evidence for climate change.	• 'World temperatures are going up all the time and winters are getting warmer.' • 'Global warming is making the seasons different and there are more floods.' • 'Scientists think more floods and storms are because of global warming.'
	0	No relevant content.	

(c) Fill in the marking table below.

Strengths of this answer	
Ways to improve this answer	
The level I would give this answer is…	**The mark I would give this answer is…**

Worked example

The sample answer in Activity 2 is marked below, so you can compare your marking with this. The text has been coloured and underlined to show the following strengths of the answer:

- Points in red
- Evidence in blue
- Explanations in orange
- Links back to the question underlined

Point: the candidate makes the point that the climate is warming

Evidence: the candidate shows how temperatures are 1°C warmer than they were 100 years ago

Explanation: the candidate briefly explains the increase

Link (evaluation): the candidate gives one reason why temperature readings may not be accurate

Globally the climate is warming, with evidence to prove that this is the case. Everywhere in the world is warmer, though seas are warming less than land. This is because greenhouse gas emissions have increased. It is hard to know exactly what temperatures were like in 1900 and more people and organisations record the weather now than at that time, so there were fewer thermometers back then. So some of the evidence could be questionable just because there were fewer recordings previously.

Point: the candidate makes a second point about temperature recordings and reliability

Link (evaluation): the candidate extends the evaluation by referring to the volume of temperature recordings

Evidence: the candidate shows evidence of sea levels rising

Even if temperature recordings are not completely reliable, there is a lot of evidence to show that sea levels are rising globally by about 20 cm in 100 years, partly because ocean water expands when it warms and so it rises. Many coastal areas are flooding more now, so it is a global process and not just evidence from one place.

Explanation: the candidate gives a reason for this

Evidence/point: the candidate makes the point about retreating glaciers

Link (evaluation): the candidate shows that this evidence is probably reliable as many places experience the same thing

Explanation: the candidate explains this

Other evidence which shows that temperatures are rising comes from retreating glaciers and ice sheets because they are melting. especially on land areas where there is expected to be an increase of at least 5°C by 2100, as shown in Figure 1. Many glaciers have been photographed for over 100 years, and many in the Alps and on Greenland show that they have retreated a long way from where they were.

Link (evaluation): the candidate refers to the reliability of photos taken over a long time to show change

✓ Examiner feedback

This is an excellent answer worth 9 marks. The student shows knowledge and understanding, but also weighs up whether the evidence for climate change is reliable.

For SPaG, the student gained all 3 marks. The answer is in paragraphs, and there is good spelling and punctuation.

Hitting Level 3

1 Know some detail

A Level 2 answer might say:

- *Globally, sea level has risen in the past century*

whereas Level 3 would say:

- *Research shows that the average global sea level has risen by 10–20 cm since 1920.*

2 Explain processes clearly, step-by-step

A Level 2 answer might say:

- *Global warming has increased temperatures, causing rising sea levels*

whereas Level 3 would say:

- *Rising global temperatures have melted ice caps and glaciers, meaning that more water goes into the sea.*

3 Use what you know to answer the question

A Level 2 answer might say:

- *Evidence that the sea level is rising comes from scientists who agree*

whereas Level 3 would say:

- *Evidence for climate change is reliable as it comes from the world's best scientists in the IPCC.*

When should I use an example or case study?

Using real places and processes is always a good idea for an exam answer. Learning about real places helps to understand complex problems, and you might find it easier to tell the examiner about real places you have learned about.

But beware! Case studies and examples are needed in only a few parts of the specification (see page 12). So follow these tips to use examples in the best way and keep your answer on track:

Keep in line with the question! Only use a detailed example if the question asks you to. For example, 'Use a case study of a major UK city' would clearly want you to write about it in detail.

Keep it brief! Don't start writing about places you've studied without knowing in advance where you're going to stop.

Keep it focused! Make sure you don't drift away from the question that you're meant to be answering – it's easy to do once you start writing about somewhere you know.

Keep it relevant! Give a simple 'for example' or 'e.g.' in your answer. In the answer on page 89, the candidate could have named somewhere where glaciers are retreating, or which are being affected by sea level rise.

Questions using 'do you agree?'

- Sometimes the command phrase is 'Do you agree?'

- It means that you should weigh up evidence that you know about, and think about whether or not the statement is true.

- Then you should make suggestions about what could happen based on the statement given and what you know and understand.

Now try this!

2. 'For those who live in low-income areas of cities in one of the world's low-income countries (LICs) or newly emerging economies (NEEs), life presents far more problems than benefits.'

Do you agree with this statement? Using **one or more** examples, explain your answer.

[9 marks]

_____

_____

_____

_____

_____

_____

_____

_____

_____

_____

_____

_____

_____

_____

_____

_____

_____

_____

Focus on Paper 3: Geographical applications
Section A: Issue evaluation

Paper 3

Time: 1 hr 15 min

Structure: Section A Issue evaluation (34 marks + 3 SPaG)

     Section B Fieldwork (36 marks + 3 SPaG)

Assessment:

- There are no options so you should attempt every question. And remember, never leave a question blank!
- There are two 9-mark questions, one at the end of each section. In Section A, this question is about decision-making. In Section B, it is a question based on your own fieldwork.
- There are no marks for factual recall. The bulk of the marks are available for the application of your knowledge and understanding. There are quite a lot of marks available for skills.

Resources booklet

Section A of Paper 3 uses a resources booklet to focus your attention on a particular issue (e.g. a proposal to construct a new reservoir). The issue will be drawn from a compulsory section of the specification.

Questions in Section A will focus on the resources in the booklet, although you will be expected to use your wider knowledge and understanding of the specification to support your answers.

When do I get the resources booklet?

Your teacher will decide when to give you a copy of the resources booklet. It may be after Easter when you have completed the course. Your teacher will guide you through the booklet and you should use labels and highlighters to pick out the key points in each resource.

Do I get a new resources booklet in the exam?

Yes. You will have a fresh copy of the resources booklet in the exam. You will **not** be allowed to take your original annotated version into the exam with you. Don't forget to take a pen, pencil, ruler, rubber and calculator!

Do I need to do any additional research?

No. You should **not** do any additional research as you will only be credited with supporting evidence that is taken from the resources booklet. Don't waste your time trawling the Internet!

Using the resources booklet

> The resources booklet contains three figures and there are six pages of resources in total. Go to pages 103–108 to see what a resources booklet looks like. Each figure will have a particular focus and may involve different types of resources (see below).

What should I do with the resources booklet?

In preparation for the exam, it is important that you are confident in using the resources booklet. You need to make sure that you understand **all** of the resources. When you first get your resources booklet:

1. Have a quick look through the booklet to identify the topic being studied.
2. Find this topic in your textbook or revision book. You will need to revise this prior to the exam to support your background knowledge and understanding.
3. For each resource, use labels/annotations and highlighters to pick out the key points:

- **For a graph,** identify the main trends and pick out some key points (highs, lows, anomalies). Make sure you understand the axes and the scales.

- **For a map,** draw rings to pick out patterns of areas with the highest and lowest values. Look for any causal reasons, such as latitude with the distribution of tropical cyclones. What's in the key? Remember to use the scale and north arrow.

- **For a photo,** look closely to pick out the key features, adding labels or drawing rings. Remember to use locational terms such as 'foreground' and 'background'.

- **For a text article,** use a highlighter to pick out key facts and figures. Consider the purpose of the article. For example, is it presenting different points of view or advantages and disadvantages? Identify and look up any words that you do not understand.

Activity 1

The map below is from **Figure 1** in the sample resources booklet (pages 103–108).

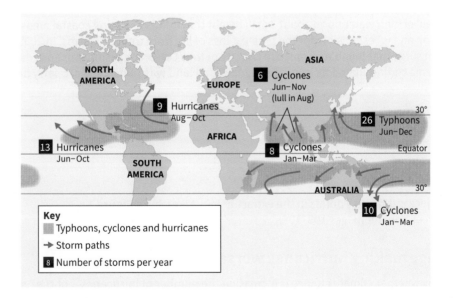

(a) Add the following labels to help you describe the distribution of tropical storms:

- Two latitudinal belts of tropical storms • Few tropical storms north of 30° • No tropical storms at the Equator

(b) Can you add one or two more labels to the map?

 **Activity 2**

The photo below is from **Figure 2** in the sample resources booklet (pages 103–108). It shows the effects of Hurricane Dorian on the Bahamas.

Using evidence in the photo, suggest and label **one of each** of the following:

(a) A social effect   **(b)** An economic effect   **(c)** An environmental effect

Worked example

Here is a section of text taken from **Figure 1** in the sample resources booklet (pages 103–108).

It has been highlighted to pick out the key points.

Storm surge

This is a surge or 'wall' of high water up to about 3 m in height that floods low-lying coastal areas. It can cause enormous devastation and is responsible for the greatest loss of life from tropical storms. In 2005, Hurricane Katrina caused a 7.6 m storm surge that inundated much of the city of New Orleans, causing immense damage and loss of life. Freshwater became contaminated by saltwater, agricultural land was ruined and property destroyed.

 **Activity 3**

Use a highlighter to pick out the key points in the extract below, taken from **Figure 1** in the sample resources booklet (pages 103–108).

Is climate change making hurricanes worse?

'Scientists cannot say whether climate change is increasing the number of hurricanes, but the ones that do happen are likely to be more powerful and more destructive because of our warming climate,' says BBC Weather's Tomasz Schafernaker. Here's why:

- An increase in sea surface temperatures strengthens the wind speeds within storms and also raises the amount of precipitation from a hurricane.
- Sea levels are expected to rise by 30 cm to 120 cm over the next century, with the potential of far worse damage from sea surges and coastal flooding during storms.

Tackling the exam questions

In Section A, you will need to answer a series of questions based on the issue in the resources booklet. To answer the questions you should use evidence from the resources together with your background knowledge and understanding.

Low-mark questions

There will be a few short-answer questions, probably worth 1 or 2 marks each. They may be skills-based (e.g. making a calculation) or may ask you to 'explain' or 'suggest'. You will probably be asked to complete a diagram.

Now try this!

Attempt the following questions based on the sample resources booklet (page 103).

1. In **Figure 1**, calculate the total number of recorded hurricanes between 1851 and 2018. **[1 mark]**

_____

2. Explain the pattern of tropical storms shown by the map in **Figure 1**. **[2 marks]**

_____

_____

_____

Extended-answer questions

There will probably be three 6-mark questions in Section A (or two 6-mark and one 4-mark). They are likely to involve some form of discussion or evaluation, using command words such as 'discuss' or 'to what extent'.

- Take time to make a plan before you start to write.
- Make sure you refer to supporting evidence from the resources.
- If relevant, refer to concepts such as scale, development and sustainability.

> **Tip** It is a good idea to use short extracts from text articles to support a point you are making. Write them in quote marks (e.g. 'immense damage and loss of life') and give a reference to the article if appropriate. Be selective – avoid simply copying out huge chunks of text!

Now try this!

3. Using **Figure 1,** explain why climate change is likely to increase the impacts of tropical storms **[4 marks]**

_____

_____

_____

_____

➡️

_____

_____

_____

_____

_____

Worked example

'A storm surge is the greatest threat associated with a tropical storm.' Discuss this statement. **[6 marks]**

A storm surge is a surge of high water that floods low-lying coastal areas. It can cause widespread devastation and destruction. In 2005, a 7 m storm surge affected New Orleans (Hurricane Katrina) causing 'immense damage and loss of life'. Other threats from tropical storms include strong winds over 120 km/h and very heavy rain (over 200 mm in a few hours). Scientists expect the threat of storm surges to increase as 'sea levels rise in the future due to climate change'.

Shows good understanding of a storm surge and its impacts

Makes good use of examples

This is a **Level 2** answer and earns **4 marks**. It lacks discussion, restricting the answer to Level 2. The command word 'discuss' requires the candidate to give both sides of an argument.

Now try this!

Attempt the following question based on the sample resources booklet (pages 103–108).

4. To what extent did the forecast track of Hurricane Dorian (30 August 2019) prove to be accurate? **[6 marks]**

_____

_____

_____

_____

_____

_____

_____

_____

_____

_____

_____

_____

Tackling the 9-mark decision-making question

The final question in Section A requires you to make and then justify a decision. Here are some important points to remember:

- There is no right or wrong answer, but you have to make a decision and then justify it using evidence from the resources booklet.
- You will be asked to tick a box to show your decision. No marks are available for your decision but it helps the examiner to mark your answer.
- Do not leave this question blank! Focus on the geography, write something sensible using evidence from the booklet, and try to offer more than one point of view (a discussion).
- SPaG provides three additional marks for this question. This is why it's so important that you attempt this question.

Before the exam

You will probably have a good idea about what the question is likely to be. This will enable you to make some basic preparations.

Look at **Figure 3** in the sample resources booklet (pages 103–108). It focuses on a proposal to construct a storm surge barrier to help protect New York from future flooding associated with tropical storms. There is information about the advantages and disadvantages of the proposal.

Given this information, it seems likely that the 9-mark question will focus on whether or not the proposal should go ahead. But you shouldn't try to guess the precise wording of the question!

> **Tip** Don't try to guess the precise wording of the 9-mark question beforehand. If you do, you may be tempted to simply rewrite the answer you have already practised. Be confident with the resources booklet and answer the question that is set in the exam.

Activity 4

Use a table to summarise information and help you prepare for the decision-making question. Notice that the table below has been split into social, economic and environmental factors. This will give you a clear structure for your answer.

(a) Complete the table below to identify advantages and disadvantages of the proposal in **Figure 3** of the sample resources booklet (pages 103–108). Try to include two points in each box.

	Advantages	Disadvantages
Social		
Economic		• Hugely expensive ($20–25 billion)
Environmental	• Impacts will be minimal (according to the Storm Surge Working Group)	

(b) Use a highlighter to pick out what you consider to be the most important points (some points are more important than others!).

Section A: Issue evaluation

In the exam

You have about 35 minutes for Section A. Try to leave yourself about 10 minutes to answer this final 9-mark question. Do not be tempted to go beyond this time limit as it will affect your performance in Section B.

- Plan your answer – use a table or make a list of the key points you want to include.
- Support your decision with evidence, using clear paragraphs (use PEEL).
- Make explicit links to the evidence in the booklet; quote information to support your argument.
- Consider the pros and cons, if appropriate.
- Write a conclusion ('In conclusion…').

> **Tip** Directly lifting information from the booklet (e.g. by copying out sentences) will gain you some low-level marks. Try instead to use the information to support an argument.

Now try this!

5. 'The City of New York authority has decided not to go ahead with the storm surge barrier system.'
   Do you think this was the right decision?

   Yes ☐

   No ☐

   Tick the box to show your choice

   Use evidence from the resources booklet and your own understanding to explain your choice.

   [9 marks] [+3 SPaG marks]

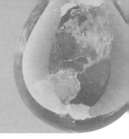

Focus on Paper 3: Geographical applications
Section B: Fieldwork

Part 1: short-answer questions based on unfamiliar fieldwork

Here you will be presented with information about fieldwork enquiries. This might take the form of photos, sketch maps, diagrams and tables of data. The questions will focus on the six stages of enquiry, shown in the table below.

	Stage of enquiry	Don't forget to revise...
1	Question selection	• Primary and secondary sources • Risk assessments
2	Data collection (methodology) including sampling techniques	• Primary and secondary data • Sampling methods (random, stratified and systematic)
3	Data presentation	• Selection of appropriate methods
4	Data analysis	• Use of appropriate statistical tests (e.g. central tendency, percentages, best fit lines)
5	Conclusions	• Links between conclusions and the original aim of enquiry
6	Evaluation	• Problems/limitations with data collection • Suggestions for other data sources • Reliability of conclusions

Be prepared to:

complete a diagram such as a bar chart or scattergraph – don't forget to use the key if asked to add shading

suggest suitable alternatives to data collection or presentation

calculate using data (e.g. median, mean, percentage)

assess the methods of data collection or reliability of conclusions

describe patterns on diagrams

suggest options or alternatives.

Now try this!

1. Using a questionnaire, students asked 100 people at random what they thought was the main problem in their local town centre. The survey was conducted at 9 a.m. on a rainy Saturday morning. **Figure 1** shows the results of the survey.

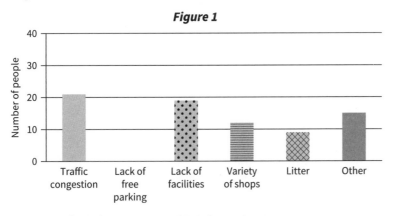

Figure 1

1.1 Complete **Figure 1** using this information:

Lack of free parking = 24 people

[2 marks]

1.2 Suggest **one** adaptation to the method used that might provide the students with more appropriate data.

[1 mark]

_____

_____

1.3 Suggest **one** additional data collection technique that the students could use to find out more about urban problems in this town centre.

[1 mark]

_____

Part 2: questions based on own fieldwork

In this part of the exam you will be asked questions on your physical and human enquiries. It's a great opportunity to write about something that you actually experienced, so make the most of it!

What questions will I be asked?

Look at **Figure 1**. These are the questions that you are most likely to be asked. Notice that there are no questions asking you to describe what you did. Instead, the questions will ask you to **explain** why you did certain things (such as the collection of data or the selection of a presentation technique).

> 💡 **Tip** Know the titles of your physical and human enquiries. You will be expected to write the titles before answering the questions.

Figure 1

Why was the question suitable for geographical study?

Why did I choose the locations?

What were the potential risks and how were they reduced?

What data did I collect?

What sampling methods did I use and why were they appropriate?

Why did I choose the presentation techniques?

Why did I use statistical techniques?

Why did I get the results/conclusion?

Why were there issues with the enquiry (evaluation)?

How to succeed in the fieldwork enquiry questions

- Revise your fieldwork enquiries thoroughly. Make sure you know what you did and, most importantly, why you did it.
- Complete revision grids (see page 102) for both fieldwork enquiries.
- Be prepared to use simple sketches to support your answers.
- You do **not** need to learn lots of facts and figures.

How to cope with the final 9-mark question

For the final question, you have to select **one** of your enquiries to write about. Think carefully about which enquiry is best suited to the question.

The question is most likely to focus on the **interrelationships** between data collection, results, conclusions and evaluation.

 **Activity 5**

The following questions will help you to see the interrelationships between different aspects of the enquiry process. This should help you to plan an answer for the 9-mark question.

For your **physical** enquiry:

(a) What were the conclusions?

_____

_____

(b) How reliable were your conclusions?

_____

_____

(c) Your results were based on your data collection. How could that have been improved so that your results were more accurate? (Hint: consider the sampling locations, number of samples, range of data collected, etc.)

_____

_____

Look at **Figure 2**, which shows interrelationships in a fieldwork enquiry. Notice how 'Data collection', 'Results' and 'Conclusion' are all linked. Try to discuss these interrelationships when answering the 9-mark question.

Figure 2

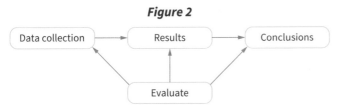

 **Activity 2**

Use the table on the next page to help you write a plan to answer this question.

> For **one** of your enquiries, to what extent did the data that you collected allow you to make reliable conclusions? **[9 marks] [+3 SPaG marks]**

Title of fieldwork enquiry: _____

Tip Do not leave the 9-mark question blank! Identify the geography, cross out any words you don't understand (to make the question simpler) and write something of relevance. By having a go, you may be awarded SPaG marks!

See, for example, how this question can be made simpler:

~~To what extent~~ did the data that you collected allow you to make ~~valid and~~ reliable conclusions?

What data did you collect?		
What were your conclusions?		
How reliable were your conclusions?		
Did your data allow you to make reliable conclusions?		
Consider 'to what extent' your data allowed you to make reliable conclusions. Place a cross on the line and use this to help you in your discussion.	No _____ Yes 0% 100%	

Now try this!

Now attempt to answer the question in Activity 2 using a separate sheet of paper.

Fieldwork enquiry revision template

	Physical enquiry	Human enquiry
Investigation title		
1. Question selection		
Why is the question suitable for geographical study?		
What are the risks and how were they reduced?		
Why were the locations chosen?		
2. Data collection (methodology) including sampling techniques		
Explain the collection of **one** form of primary data (sampling, methods, location, etc.)*		
Explain a **second** method of data collection (primary or secondary)		
3. Data presentation		
For **one** presentation method, why did you choose it to present fieldwork data?*		
For **a second** presentation method, why did you choose it to present fieldwork data?		
4. Data analysis		
What statistical techniques did you use and why?		
What were your main results? Were there any anomalies?		
5. Conclusions		
What were your conclusions?		
6. Evaluation		
What were the problems/limitations with data collection? (Methods, locations, timings, actual data, etc.)		
What other data might have been useful in answering the question?		
How reliable were the conclusions?		

* You will probably only be asked to write about **one** primary data collection method and **one** method of data presentation. However, it is useful to prepare **two** so that you can select the best one to use when answering a question.

Figure 1

Tropical storm development, distribution and impacts

What is a tropical storm?

A tropical storm is a huge storm that develops in the tropics. In the USA and the Caribbean these are commonly called **hurricanes**. In South-East Asia and Australia they are usually called **cyclones**, but in Japan and the Philippines they are called **typhoons**.

Distribution of tropical storms

The world map shows the regions where most tropical storms form, as well as their principal months of occurrence and the most common tracks they follow. Tropical storms do not develop within about 5° of the Equator because the effect of the Earth's rotation, which triggers the 'spin' of a tropical storm, is too weak. Surface ocean temperatures exceeding 26.5°C are required for them to form and, for this reason, they seldom form poleward of 30° latitude nor over the cool waters of the South Atlantic and the eastern South Pacific.

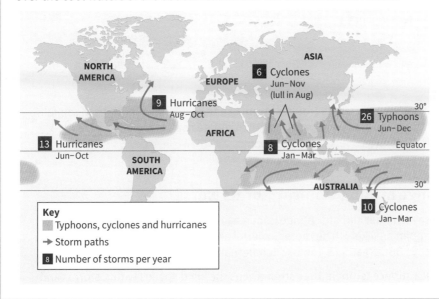

Total number of tropical storms by month (1851–2018)

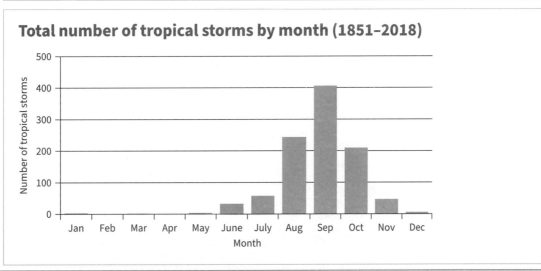

Tropical storm hazards

Tropical storms bring a deadly mix of high seas, strong winds and torrential rain. A huge proportion of the world's population lives near the coast, so there is a significant potential for loss of life and property damage.

Strong winds

Average wind speeds exceed 120 km/h (75 mph). The strongest winds occur at the eyewall (the outer edge of the eye) where they can reach 250 km/h. The strong winds are capable of causing significant damage and disruption by tearing off roofs, breaking windows and damaging communication networks, often causing power cuts.

Storm surge

This is a surge or 'wall' of high water up to about 3 m in height that floods low-lying coastal areas. It can cause enormous devastation and is responsible for the greatest loss of life from tropical storms. In 2005, Hurricane Katrina caused a 7.6 m storm surge that inundated much of the city of New Orleans, causing immense damage and loss of life. Freshwater became contaminated by saltwater, agricultural land was ruined and property destroyed.

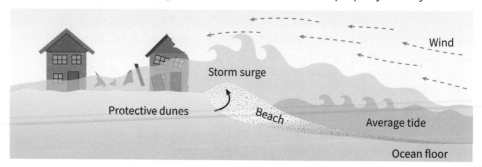

Torrential rainfall

The warm, humid air associated with a tropical storm can trigger huge quantities of rainfall, often exceeding 200 mm in just a few hours. This can inundate coastal regions and lead to catastrophic flooding inland as rivers burst their banks.

Is climate change making tropical storms worse?

'Scientists cannot say whether climate change is increasing the number of hurricanes, but the ones that do happen are likely to be more powerful and more destructive because of our warming climate,' says BBC Weather's Tomasz Schafernaker. Here's why:

- An increase in sea surface temperatures strengthens the wind speeds within storms and also raises the amount of precipitation from a tropical storm.
- Sea levels are expected to rise by 30 cm to 120 cm over the next century, with the potential of far worse damage from sea surges and coastal flooding during storms.

More strong Atlantic hurricanes: the effect of climate change?

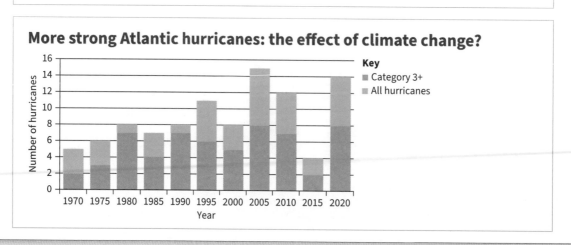

Figure 2

Hurricane Dorian, the Bahamas, 2019

The impacts of Hurricane Dorian

Tropical storms are incredibly powerful and can cause devastation to small islands and coastal regions. In 2019, the Bahamas was struck by Hurricane Dorian, the most powerful hurricane to hit the islands on record. Regarded as the worst natural disaster in the country's history, Hurricane Dorian killed over 50 people and devastated huge swathes of the country, causing damage worth over $7 billion.

The hurricane made landfall on 1 September and battered the Abaco Islands and Grand Bahama, in the north of the archipelago, for two days. Winds reaching 165 km/h combined with a powerful storm surge and torrential rainfall caused almost total destruction of harbours, residential property and agricultural land. One of the main reasons for the extensive devastation was the unusually slow speed of movement of the storm, causing huge quantities of rainfall. Many people were evacuated from coastal properties, most of which were destroyed by the storm. Power lines were brought down and roads were flooded, hampering rescue efforts.

Damage caused by Hurricane Dorian on Grand Bahama

Extract from *The Washington Post*

Classified as a Category 5 hurricane, Dorian is the most powerful storm to affect the Bahamas. Its sustained winds – reaching 185 mph – are close to the highest ever recorded in the Atlantic Ocean.

Satellite images reveal Hurricane Dorian to be almost perfectly symmetrical, with its distinctive eye surrounded by towering, swirling thunderstorm clouds. The clouds surrounding the eye resemble the fiery streaks of a Catherine wheel firework.

Dorian's winds are unusually strong for a storm so far north in the Atlantic Ocean. Its central pressure, recorded at 911 mb, is lower than Hurricane Andrew's, the last great storm to strike southern Florida in 1992. Since 1950, the strength of Dorian's winds is surpassed only by the 190 mph winds associated with Hurricane Allen in 1980.

Satellite image of Hurricane Dorian approaching the northern Bahamas and threatening Florida

Tracking Hurricane Dorian

The map below shows the predicted track and strength of Hurricane Dorian, forecast on 30 August 2019. Forecasters expected the hurricane to intensify rapidly as it headed towards the Bahamas. It was then expected to make landfall in central Florida, threatening strong winds (over 85 mph), torrential rain and a storm surge.

Hurricane Dorian forecast track (30 August 2019)

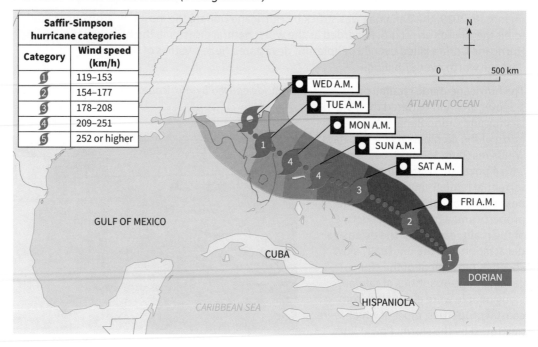

Saffir-Simpson hurricane categories	
Category	**Wind speed (km/h)**
1	119–153
2	154–177
3	178–208
4	209–251
5	252 or higher

Threats to the USA's East Coast and New York

By 1 September, forecasters amended the predicted track of Hurricane Dorian, suggesting that it would not make landfall in Florida but would instead track parallel to the coastline.

This turned out to be an accurate forecast, with the storm passing close to the coastline of Florida and North Carolina. The storm then passed dangerously close to the coast of New Jersey and Delaware, with heavy rain falling on New York City.

This rekindled memories of the devastating impacts of Hurricane Sandy on the New Jersey coast and New York City in 2012. Had the hurricane tracked a little further west, the impacts could have been considerable.

Hurricane Dorian eventually made landfall in Nova Scotia, Canada on 7 September 2019.

Figure 3

New York: under threat from hurricanes

The East Coast of the USA, from Florida in the south to New England in the north, is vulnerable to the effects of hurricanes. Much of the coastline is flat and low-lying, comprising sandy barrier islands, wide beaches and extensive river estuaries. To combat the threat of hurricanes, most communities rely upon prediction and planning, evacuating people away from coastal areas to temporary shelters.

In 2012, Hurricane Sandy struck the New Jersey coast, devastating several coastal communities and driving a storm surge into New York Bay that caused significant damage and financial losses in New York City itself. This was just a year after Hurricane Irene had struck the city, causing widespread flooding.

Impacts of Hurricane Sandy in New York (2012)
• 53 people died and thousands were evacuated.
• Thousands of homes and 250 000 vehicles were destroyed.
• $19 billion damage caused; the Stock Exchange closed for two days.
• Fire at Breezy Point, caused by an exploding transmitter, destroyed over 100 buildings.
• Subways and road tunnels were flooded; international airports were closed.
• Several hospitals were temporarily closed due to flooding.

With sea levels rising due to climate change and an increase in hurricane intensity, large parts of New York and New Jersey are likely to be at risk in the future. The National Oceanic and Atmospheric Administration (NOAA) has recorded a sea level rise of about 30 cm per century. By the end of the century, sea level is expected to rise by 100–200 cm.

The New York/New Jersey Metropolitan Storm Surge Working Group's proposal

In the wake of Hurricane Sandy, a group of scientists, business leaders, engineers, lawyers and civic leaders established the New York/New Jersey Metropolitan Storm Surge Working Group. They have proposed a series of storm surge barriers to protect vulnerable seaports, international airports, subway and road tunnels, hospitals and millions of low-income residents living on low-lying land.

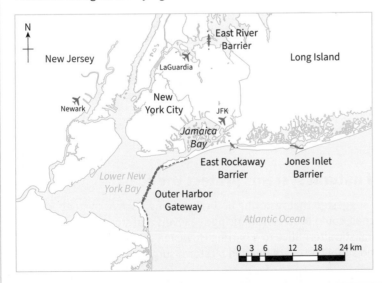

Research has suggested that rising sea levels and more powerful hurricanes will increase the flood risk significantly. Floods of a magnitude that used to occur on average once every 500 years pre-1800 now occur once every 24 years and, by 2050, are predicted to occur once every 5 years.

Storm surge barriers have been constructed elsewhere. Three barriers have operated successfully in New England and, in Europe, the Thames Barrier (UK), Delta Project (the Netherlands) and St Petersburg Dam (Russia) have prevented the flooding of vulnerable areas.

Part of the St Petersburg Dam, Russia

The Aerts' Report on the storm surge barrier system

Unconvinced by the plans and concerned about costs, New York City commissioned a report by Dr Jeroen Aerts of the University of Amsterdam. Asked to compare the barrier system with less ambitious improvements such as raising levées (river banks), relocating subway stations, constructing smaller local barriers and raising key buildings, Aerts concluded that the costs/benefits were roughly equal.

Despite this, the City authorities dismissed the large-scale project on the following grounds:

- The system of barriers would be hugely expensive ($20–25 billion).
- The sheer scale of the barriers could mean that they take decades to construct.
- The impact on fish migration, water quality and shoreline processes are unknown.
- Massive levées would dramatically affect local communities and the character of natural beaches.
- Spending on barriers would divert money from other schemes to mitigate sea level rise.

Aerts reacted to the decision with surprise, suggesting that planning should start now to protect the city in the future. 'As a Dutchman,' Aerts said, 'you are quite surprised to see a large city like New York – so many people exposed – and no levées, no protection at all. [That] was astonishing to me. Don't rule out the barriers yet... you need a barrier.'

Storm Surge Working Group responses to the decision

> The small-scale projects have yet to be designed, let alone constructed.

> The impact on natural systems will be minimal as most of the time the barriers would be open. Environmental impacts will be minimal as long as the floodgates are open 60–80% of the time.

> Local plans already involve the construction of levées, affecting the character of beaches.

> The project could be expanded in the future to protect Long Island and the New Jersey coast.

Can the restoration of natural systems protect the coast?

Local environmentalists have suggested that restoring natural systems, such as oyster beds, coastal wetlands and sand dunes, could protect from rising sea levels and storm surges. This would be a cheap, more naturalistic alternative to a barrier. However, scientists have suggested that these environments would simply be overwhelmed by storm surges so would be largely ineffective.

Specification checklist

Tick or colour the appropriate box to indicate your confidence level with the key ideas from each specification topic listed below.

Specification topic	Key ideas	☺	😐	☹
1 Natural hazards	Natural hazards pose major risks to people and property			
2 Tectonic hazards	Earthquakes and volcanic eruptions are the result of physical processes			
	The effects of, and responses to, tectonic hazards vary between areas of contrasting levels of wealth			
	Management can reduce the effects of tectonic hazards			
3 Weather hazards	Global atmospheric circulation helps to determine patterns of weather and climate			
	Tropical storms (hurricanes, cyclones, typhoons) develop as a result of particular physical conditions			
	Tropical storms have significant effects on people and the environment			
	The UK is affected by a number of weather hazards			
	Extreme weather events in the UK have impacts on human activity			
4 Climate change	Climate change is the result of natural and human factors and has a range of effects			
	Managing climate change involves both mitigation (reducing causes) and adaptation (responding to change)			
5 Ecosystems	Ecosystems exist at a range of scales and involve the interaction between living and non-living components			
6 Tropical rainforests	Tropical rainforests have distinctive environmental characteristics			
	Deforestation has economic and environmental impacts			
	Tropical rainforests need to be managed to be sustainable			
7 Hot deserts	Hot desert ecosystems have distinctive environmental characteristics			
	Development of hot desert environments creates opportunities and challenges			
	Areas on the fringe of hot deserts are at risk of desertification			
8 Cold environments	Cold environments (polar and tundra) have distinctive characteristics			
	Development of cold environments creates opportunities and challenges			
	Cold environments are at risk from economic development			
9 UK landscapes	The UK has a range of diverse landscapes			
10 Coastal landscapes	The coast is shaped by a number of physical processes			
	Distinctive coastal landforms are the result of rock type, structure and physical processes			
	Different management strategies can be used to protect coastlines from the effects of physical processes			
11 River landscapes	The shape of river valleys changes as rivers flow downstream			
	Distinctive fluvial (river) landforms result from different physical processes			
	Different management strategies can be used to protect river landscapes from the effects of flooding			

12 Glacial landscapes	Ice was a powerful force in shaping the physical landscape of the UK			
	Distinctive global landforms result from different physical processes			
	Glaciated upland areas provide opportunities for different economic activities, and management strategies can be used to reduce land use conflicts			
13 The urban world	A growing percentage of the world's population lives in urban areas			
	Urban growth creates opportunities and challenges for cities in lower income countries and newly emerging economies			
14 Urban change in the UK	Urban change in cities in the UK leads to a variety of social, economic and environmental opportunities and challenges			
15 Sustainable urban development	Urban sustainability requires management of resources and transport			
16 The development gap	There are global variations in economic development and quality of life			
	Various strategies exist for reducing the global development gap			
17 Nigeria: a newly emerging economy	Some LICs or NEEs are experiencing rapid economic development, which leads to a significant social, environmental and cultural change			
18 The changing UK economy	Major changes in the economy of the UK have affected, and will continue to affect, employment patterns and regional growth			
19 Resource management	Food, water and energy are fundamental to human development			
	The changing demand and provision of resources in the UK create opportunities and challenges			
20 Food management	Demand for food resources is rising globally but supply can be insecure, which may lead to conflict			
	Different strategies can be used to increase food supply			
21 Water management	Demand for water resources is rising globally but supply can be insecure, which may lead to conflict			
	Different strategies can be used to increase water supply			
22 Energy management	Demand for energy resources is rising globally but supply can be insecure, which may lead to conflict			
	Different strategies can be used to increase energy supply			
23 Issue evaluation				
24 Fieldwork	Physical geography topic			
	Human geography topic			
	Unfamiliar fieldwork			

Skills and case studies checklists

Tick or colour the appropriate box to indicate your confidence level with the geographical skills listed below.

	☺	😐	☹
Cartographic skills – atlas maps			
Coordinates – latitude and longitude			
Distributions and patterns of human and physical features, e.g. population distribution and movements, transport, settlements, relief, drainage			
Interrelationships between physical and human features and patterns on thematic maps			
Cartographic skills – Ordnance Survey maps			
Interpret at a range of scales, including 1:50 000 and 1:25 000			
Four- and six-figure grid references			
Scale, distance and direction (straight and curved line distances with a variety of scales)			
Gradient, contour and spot height			
Numerical and statistical information			
Basic landscape features and their characteristics			
Major relief features in relation to cross-sectional drawings			
What patterns of relief, drainage, settlement, communication and land use tell us about the physical and human landscape			
Cross-sections and transects of physical and human landscapes			
Physical features of coastlines, river and glacial landscapes			
Human activity, including tourism			
Cartographic skills – maps and photographs			
Compare maps			
Sketch maps: draw, label, understand and interpret			
Photographs: use and interpret ground, aerial and satellite photos			
Describe human and physical landscapes (landforms, vegetation, land use, settlement) and geographical phenomena from photos			
Draw sketches from photos			
Label and annotate diagrams, maps, graphs, sketches and photos			
Graphical skills			
Construct line charts, bar charts, pie charts, pictograms, histograms with equal class intervals, divided bar, scattergraphs and population pyramids			
Suggest an appropriate form of graphical representation for data			
Complete choropleth maps, isoline maps, dot maps, desire lines, proportional symbols and flow lines			
Gradient, contour and value on isoline maps			
Plot information on graphs			
Interpret population pyramids, choropleth maps, flow line maps, dispersion graphs			
Numerical skills			
Understand number, area and scales and the qualitative relationships between units			
Design fieldwork data collection sheets and collect data with an understanding of accuracy, sample size and procedures, control groups and reliability			
Proportion and ratio, magnitude and frequency			
Draw informed conclusions from numerical data			

Statistical skills			
Measures of central tendency, spread and cumulative frequency (median, mean, range, quartiles and inter-quartile range, mode and modal class)			
Calculate percentage change and understand percentiles			
Sketch trend lines through scatter plots, draw estimated lines of best fit, identify trends, make predictions			
Identify weaknesses in statistical presentation of data			
Qualitative and quantitative data Obtain, illustrate, communicate, interpret, analyse and evaluate geographical information from primary and secondary sources including:			
Maps			
Fieldwork data			
Geospatial data presented in GIS frameworks			
Satellite imagery			
Written and digital sources			
Visual and graphical sources			
Numerical and statistical information			
Formulate enquiry and argument			
Identify questions and sequences of enquiry			
Write descriptively, analytically and critically			
Communicate your ideas effectively			
Develop an extended written argument			
Draw well-evidenced and informed conclusions			
Literacy			
Communicate information in ways suitable for a range of target audiences			

Fill in your examples and case studies to use as a revision checklist.

Theme	Example (Ex)/case study (CS) needed	My example/case study
Challenge of natural hazards	• **Ex:** Tectonic hazard, two contrasting countries (effects and responses) • **Ex:** Tropical storm (effects and responses) • **Ex:** Recent extreme weather event in the UK (causes, impacts and management)	
The living world	• **Ex:** Small-scale UK ecosystem • **CS:** Tropical rainforest (causes of deforestation, impacts and issues) • **CS:** Development opportunities and challenges in hot deserts or cold environments	
Physical landscapes in the UK	• **Ex (2):** Section of river valley/coastline/glaciated area (landforms of erosion and deposition) • **Ex (2):** River management/coastal management/tourism and management (glaciation)	
Urban issues and challenges	• **CS:** Major city in LIC/NEE (growth, opportunities, challenges) • **Ex:** Urban planning improving urban poor • **CS:** Major city in UK (migration, opportunities, challenges) • **Ex:** UK urban regeneration	
Changing economic world	• **CS:** LIC/NEE country (economic structure, TNCs, trade, aid, debt) • **Ex:** Tourism in one LIC/NEE • **Ex:** UK industrial sustainability	
Challenge of resource management	• **Ex – food (2):** Large-scale agricultural development, local scheme to increase sustainable production • **Ex – water (2):** Large-scale water transfer, local scheme to improve water supply • **Ex – energy (2):** Fossil fuels; local renewable energy	

GCSE 9-1 Geography AQA
Practice Paper

Paper 1 Living with the physical environment

Time allowed: 1 hour 30 minutes
Total number of marks: 88 (including 3 marks for spelling, punctuation, grammar and specialist terminology [SPaG])

Instructions
Answer **all** questions in Section A and Section B
Answer **two** questions in Section C

Mark schemes for the exam papers can be found at **www.oxfordsecondary.com/geog-aqa-answers**.

Exam practice papers, Paper 1 113

Section A The challenge of natural hazards

Answer **all** questions in this section.

Question 1   **The challenge of natural hazards**

| 0 | 1 | · | 1 | What is meant by a natural hazard?

[1 mark]

_____

_____

| 0 | 1 | · | 2 | Name **three** types of natural hazard.

[3 marks]

1 _____

2 _____

3 _____

| 0 | 1 | · | 3 | Explain why people continue to live in areas that are at risk from tectonic hazards.

[4 marks]

_____

_____

_____

_____

_____

_____

_____

Mark schemes for the exam papers can be found at **www.oxfordsecondary.com/geog-aqa-answers**.

Study **Figure 1**, a diagram of global atmospheric circulation

Figure 1

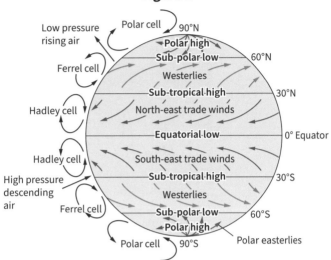

0 1 · 4   Using **Figure 1**, which **one** of the following statements is true?
Shade **one** circle.

A   Winds blow from low to high pressure.   ◯

B   High pressure is an area of sinking air.   ◯

C   The south-east trade winds blow in the northern hemisphere.   ◯

D   Surface winds are named after the direction they are blowing towards.   ◯

[1 mark]

0 1 · 5   In which wind belt shown in **Figure 1** does the UK lie?

[1 mark]

_____

0 1 · 6   Using **Figure 1**, complete the following paragraph about the
global atmospheric circulation.

[2 marks]

Pressure belts and winds move due to the position of the overhead _____.

These move _____ during the UK's winter.

Mark schemes for the exam papers can be found at **www.oxfordsecondary.com/geog-aqa-answers**.

Exam practice papers, Paper 1   115

Study **Figure 2**, a graph showing the number of tropical storms in the Atlantic between 1900 and 2018.

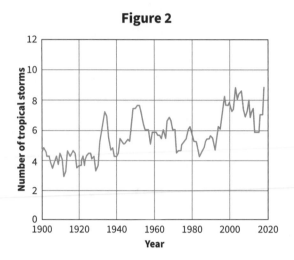

Figure 2

0 1 · 7 Outline the overall change that has occurred in the number of storms experienced in the period shown in **Figure 2**.

[1 mark]

_____

0 1 · 8 Give **two** reasons why most tropical storms develop between 5° and 15° north and south of the Equator.

[2 marks]

1 _____

_____

2 _____

_____

0 1 · 9 Explain how climate change can affect the frequency and intensity of tropical storms.

[6 marks]

_____

_____

_____

_____

_____

_____

Mark schemes for the exam papers can be found at **www.oxfordsecondary.com/geog-aqa-answers**.

| 0 | 1 | · | 10 |

'Managing climate change needs to be a combination of mitigation and adaptation.'
Do you agree with this statement? Explain your answer.

[9 marks]

[+3 SPaG marks]

Mark schemes for the exam papers can be found at **www.oxfordsecondary.com/geog-aqa-answers**.

Exam practice papers, Paper 1   117

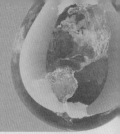

Answer **all** questions in this section.

Question 2   **The living world**

Study **Figure 3**, a photograph taken in the Cambodian tropical rainforests in South-East Asia.

Figure 3

0 2 · 1 Which **one** of the following features of a tropical rainforest is shown in **Figure 3**? Shade **one** circle only.

A   An epiphyte   ○

B   The canopy   ○

C   A buttress root   ○

D   A liana   ○

[1 mark]

0 2 · 2 Explain how the feature selected in **Figure 3** helps the vegetation adapt to the climate of the tropical rainforests.

[2 marks]

_____

_____

_____

_____

Mark schemes for the exam papers can be found at **www.oxfordsecondary.com/geog-aqa-answers**.

118   **Exam practice papers, Paper 1**

Study **Figure 4**, a diagram showing the food web in a tropical rainforest.

Figure 4

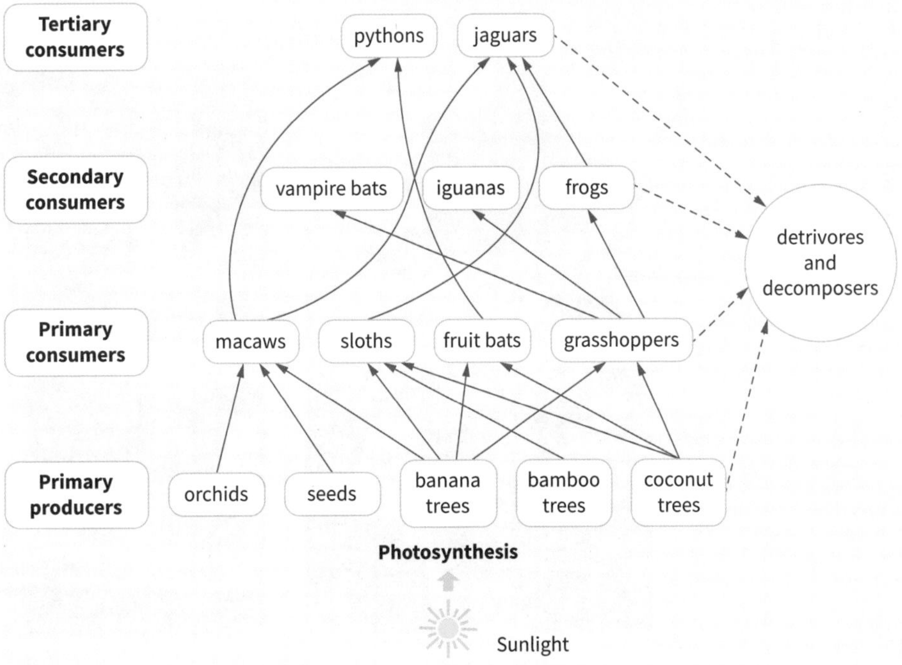

0 2 · 3   With the help of **Figure 4**, which one of the following are primary consumers?
Shade one circle only.

A   Herbivores

B   Carnivores

C   Top carnivores

D   Decomposers

[1 mark]

0 2 · 4   Explain why the number of species reduces when moving through the different layers
of the food web from the primary producers up to the tertiary consumers, as shown
in **Figure 4**.

[2 marks]

_____

_____

_____

_____

Mark schemes for the exam papers can be found at **www.oxfordsecondary.com/geog-aqa-answers**.

Exam practice papers, Paper 1   119

Study **Figure 5**, which shows some animals that live in tropical rainforests and a list of some of the ways animals have adapted to living in these areas in order to survive.

Adaptations

Figure 5

- Camouflage
- Sleeping throughout the day
- Having a very specialist diet
- Living in the forest canopy

0 2 · 5 Use **Figure 5** and your own understanding to explain how animals have adapted to the physical conditions of the tropical rainforests.

[6 marks]

_____

_____

_____

_____

_____

_____

_____

_____

_____

_____

_____

Mark schemes for the exam papers can be found at **www.oxfordsecondary.com/geog-aqa-answers**.

120 **Exam practice papers, Paper 1**

0 2 · 6 Study **Figure 6**, a table showing the amount of forest lost in the Amazon Basin in km^2 2012–2021.

Figure 6

Year	2012	2013	2014	2015	2016	2017	2018	2019	2020	2021
Area (km²)	4571	5891	5010	6207	7893	6947	7536	9762	8426	10476

Which year saw the smallest amount of forest lost in the period 2012–2021?

[1 mark]

_____

0 2 · 7 What was the percentage increase in the amount of forest lost between 2012 and 2021? Give your answer to the nearest whole percentage.

[2 marks]

Show your working.

Nearest whole percentage =

0 2 · 8 Calculate the mean annual amount of forest lost in km^2 in the Amazon during the period 2012–2021. Give your answer to one decimal point.

[1 mark]

_____

_____

0 2 · 9 Assess the importance of the interdependence of the climate, soils and people in **either** a hot desert environment **or** a cold environment.

[9 marks]

_____

_____

_____

_____

_____

_____

_____

_____

_____

_____

Mark schemes for the exam papers can be found at **www.oxfordsecondary.com/geog-aqa-answers**.

Extra space

Mark schemes for the exam papers can be found at **www.oxfordsecondary.com/geog-aqa-answers**.

122 **Exam practice papers, Paper 1**

Section C Physical landscapes in the UK

Answer **two** questions from the following:
Question 3 (Coasts), Question 4 (Rivers), Question 5 (Glacial).

Question 3   **Coastal landscapes in the UK**

Study **Figure 7**, a map showing the major upland areas, lowland areas and river systems of the British Isles.

Figure 7

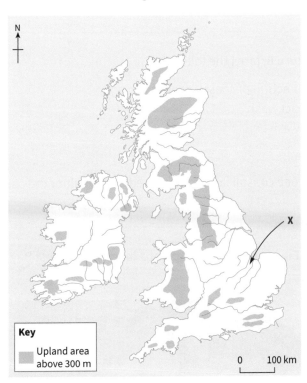

Key

Upland area above 300 m

0   100 km

| 0 | 3 | · | 1 |

What is the name of lowland area **X** shown in **Figure 7**?
Shade **one** circle only.

A   Central Lowlands of Scotland ⬭

B   The Fens ⬭

C   Vale of York ⬭

D   Vale of Glamorgan ⬭

[1 mark]

Mark schemes for the exam papers can be found at **www.oxfordsecondary.com/geog-aqa-answers**.

Exam practice papers, Paper 1   123

Study **Figure 8**, a diagram of a coastal process.

Figure 8

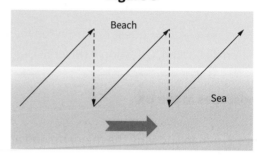

0 3 · 2   Give the name of this coastal process.

[1 mark]

_____

0 3 · 3   On **Figure 8**, label the following:

- direction of coastal process
- backwash
- swash

[2 marks]

0 3 · 4   Name one coastal landform formed as a result of the coastal process shown in **Figure 8**.

[1 mark]

_____

Study **Figure 9**, a photograph of a landslide at West Bay in Dorset.

Figure 9

Mark schemes for the exam papers can be found at **www.oxfordsecondary.com/geog-aqa-answers**.

| 0 | 3 | · | 5 |

Using **Figure 9** and your own understanding, explain how mass movement can affect the shape of the coastline.

[4 marks]

_____

_____

_____

_____

_____

_____

_____

| 0 | 3 | · | 6 |

Name an example of a coastal management scheme in the UK.

_____

Assess whether the overall benefits outweigh any conflicts that are caused as a result of the scheme.

[6 marks]

_____

_____

_____

_____

_____

_____

_____

_____

_____

_____

_____

Mark schemes for the exam papers can be found at **www.oxfordsecondary.com/geog-aqa-answers**.

Question 4   River landscapes in the UK

Study **Figure 10**, a map showing the major upland areas, lowland areas and river systems of the British Isles.

Figure 10

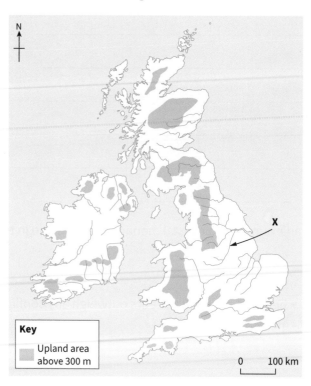

Key

▨ Upland area above 300 m

0   100 km

| 0 | 4 | · | 1 |

What is the name of river **X** shown in **Figure 10**?
Shade **one** circle only.

A   River Lagan   ◯

B   River Thames   ◯

C   River Severn   ◯

D   River Trent   ◯

[1 mark]

Mark schemes for the exam papers can be found at **www.oxfordsecondary.com/geog-aqa-answers**.

Study **Figure 11**, a diagram showing three river processes.

Figure 11

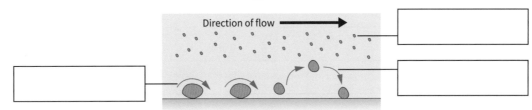

Direction of flow

River bed

0 4 · 2 On **Figure 11**, label the following:

- saltation
- suspension
- traction

[2 marks]

0 4 · 3 Name the river action these three processes perform.

[1 mark]

Study **Figure 12**, a photograph showing part of the lower course of a river.

Figure 12

Y

0 4 · 4 Name the river feature labelled 'Y' on **Figure 12**.

[1 mark]

Mark schemes for the exam papers can be found at **www.oxfordsecondary.com/geog-aqa-answers**.

Exam practice papers, Paper 1   127

| 0 | 4 | · | 5 |

Using **Figure 12** and your own understanding, explain how the river contributes to the shape of the landscape.

[4 marks]

_____

_____

_____

_____

_____

_____

_____

| 0 | 4 | · | 6 |

Name an example of a flood management scheme in the UK.

_____

Assess whether the overall benefits outweigh any environmental issues that are caused as a result of the scheme.

[6 marks]

_____

_____

_____

_____

_____

_____

_____

_____

_____

_____

Mark schemes for the exam papers can be found at **www.oxfordsecondary.com/geog-aqa-answers**.

Question 5   **Glacial landscapes in the UK**

Study **Figure 13**, a map showing the major upland areas, lowland areas and river systems of the British Isles.

Figure 13

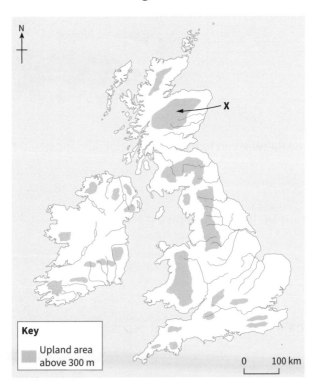

Key

▨ Upland area above 300 m

0   100 km

| 0 | 5 | · | 1 |

What is the name of upland **X** shown in **Figure 13**?
Shade **one** circle only.

A   Pennines   ⬭

B   Lake District   ⬭

C   Snowdonia   ⬭

D   Grampians   ⬭

[1 mark]

Mark schemes for the exam papers can be found at **www.oxfordsecondary.com/geog-aqa-answers**.

Exam practice papers, Paper 1   **129**

Study **Figure 14**, a diagram showing areas of glacial deposition.

Figure 14

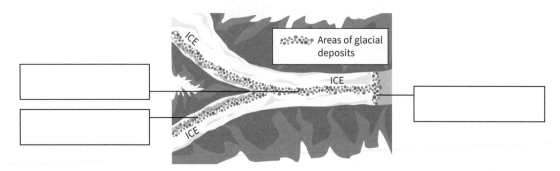

0 5 · 2 State the name given to the areas of glacial deposits in **Figure 14**.

[1 mark]

_____

0 5 · 3 On **Figure 14**, label the following glacial deposits:

- lateral
- medial
- terminal

[2 marks]

0 5 · 4 Give **one** characteristic of glacial deposits.

[1 mark]

_____

Study **Figure 15**, a photograph showing a glaciated highland area.

Figure 15

Mark schemes for the exam papers can be found at **www.oxfordsecondary.com/geog-aqa-answers**.

0 5 · 5 Using **Figure 15** and your own understanding, explain how glaciation has affected the shape of the landscape.

[4 marks]

_____

_____

_____

_____

_____

_____

_____

0 5 · 6 Name an example of a glaciated upland area in the UK used for tourism.

_____

Assess whether the overall benefits outweigh any environmental damage that is caused as a result of tourism.

[6 marks]

_____

_____

_____

_____

_____

_____

_____

_____

_____

_____

_____

Mark schemes for the exam papers can be found at **www.oxfordsecondary.com/geog-aqa-answers**.

Exam practice papers, Paper 1   131

GCSE 9-1 Geography AQA
Practice Paper

Paper 2 Challenges in the human environment

Time allowed: 1 hour 30 minutes
Total number of marks: 88 (including 3 marks for spelling, punctuation, grammar and specialist terminology [SPaG])

Instructions

Answer **all** questions in Section A and Section B
Answer question 3 and **one other** question in Section C

Mark schemes for the exam papers can be found at **www.oxfordsecondary.com/geog-aqa-answers**.

132 Exam practice papers, Paper 2

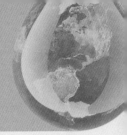

Paper 2 Challenges in the human environment
Section A Urban issues and challenges

Answer **all** questions in this section.

Question 1   **Urban issues and challenges**

Study **Figure 1**, showing the population change in a major world city, 1950–2020.

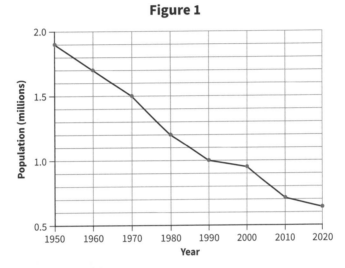

Figure 1

| 0 | 1 | · | 1 | What was the population of the city in 1970?

[1 mark]

| 0 | 1 | · | 2 | What was the change in the population between 1950 and 2020?

[1 mark]

| 0 | 1 | · | 3 | In which type of country is this city likely to be situated? Shade **one** circle only.

    A   Newly emerging economy (NEE)

    B   High-income country (HIC)

    C   Low-income country (LIC)

[1 mark]

| 0 | 1 | · | 4 | Which of the following could be a reason for the trend shown in **Figure 1**? Shade **one** circle only.

    A   There has been rural–urban migration.

    B   Birth rates have been higher than death rates.

    C   Deindustrialisation has taken place.

    D   Urbanisation is taking place.

[1 mark]

Mark schemes for the exam papers can be found at **www.oxfordsecondary.com/geog-aqa-answers**.

Study **Figure 2**, which gives information about Dharavi, a squatter settlement in the Indian city of Mumbai.

Figure 2

People		Hygiene and health	
Population of Dharavi	Estimated 800 000–1 million	No of individual toilets in Dharavi	1440
Area	2.39 km² (the size of London's Hyde Park)	People per individual toilet	625
Population density	At least 330 000 people per km²	% of women with anaemia*	75%
No of homes in Dharavi	60 000	% of women with malnutrition	50%
People per home	Between 13 and 17	% of women with recurrent gastroenteritis**	50%
Average size of home	10 m² (equivalent to a medium-sized bedroom)	Most common causes of death	Malnutrition, diarrhoea, dehydration, typhoid

anaemia: a lack of iron leading to tiredness
** gastroenteritis symptoms: diarrhoea, vomiting

0 1 · 5 Using **Figure 2**, explain why urban growth in LICs and NEEs often leads to serious challenges for the city.

[4 marks]

_____

_____

_____

_____

_____

_____

_____

_____

0 1 · 6 Discuss the attempts of a city in an LIC or an NEE to provide sufficient health and education services for its inhabitants.

[6 marks]

Name of city in LIC or NEE _____

_____

_____

_____

Mark schemes for the exam papers can be found at **www.oxfordsecondary.com/geog-aqa-answers**.

_____

_____

_____

_____

_____

_____

_____

_____

_____

Study **Figure 3**, a map showing the distribution of Asian-Indian British residents in London.

Figure 3

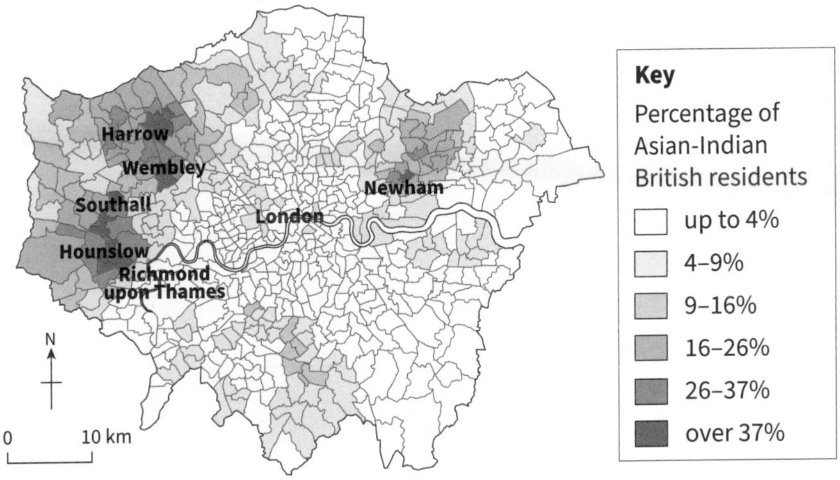

Key

Percentage of Asian-Indian British residents

☐ up to 4%

4–9%

9–16%

16–26%

26–37%

over 37%

| 0 | 1 | · | 7 | What kind of map is shown in **Figure 3**? |

[1 mark]

_____

| 0 | 1 | · | 8 | Using **Figure 3**, describe the distribution of Asian-Indian British residents in London. |

[2 marks]

_____

_____

_____

_____

Mark schemes for the exam papers can be found at **www.oxfordsecondary.com/geog-aqa-answers**.

Exam practice papers, Paper 2   135

0 1 · 9 Explain how migration can affect a city under the following headings:

[4 marks]

Enriching a city's cultural life _____

_____

_____

_____

Challenge of integration into the wider community _____

_____

_____

_____

0 1 · 10 To what extent has urban change created social and economic challenges in a UK city you have studied?

[9 marks]

[+3 SPaG marks]

Name of UK city _____

_____

_____

_____

_____

_____

_____

_____

_____

_____

_____

_____

_____

_____

_____

Continue your answer on a separate sheet of paper

Mark schemes for the exam papers can be found at **www.oxfordsecondary.com/geog-aqa-answers**.

Section B The changing economic world

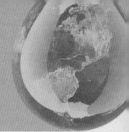

Answer **all** questions in this section.

Question 2   **The changing economic world**

Study **Figure 4**, a partly completed diagram of the five stages of the Demographic Transition Model.

Figure 4

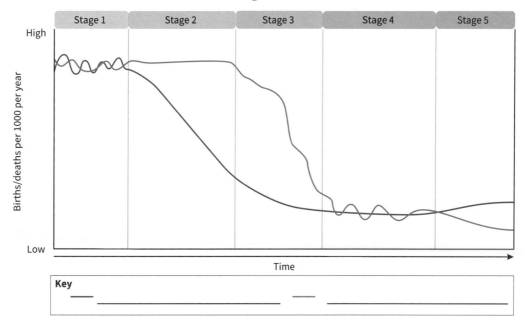

0 2 · 1 On **Figure 4**, complete the key by adding 'Birth rate' and 'Death rate' to the correct line symbol.

[1 mark]

0 2 · 2 On **Figure 4**, which stage has the greatest population increase?

A   Stage 1   ⬭
B   Stage 2   ⬭
C   Stage 3   ⬭
D   Stage 4   ⬭

[1 mark]

0 2 · 3 Complete the table to show which is the most likely stage that the following types of country have reached.

Type of country	Stage
HIC	
LIC	
NEE	

[3 marks]

Mark schemes for the exam papers can be found at **www.oxfordsecondary.com/geog-aqa-answers**.

0 2 · 4 Explain how **physical** factors can cause uneven development.

[4 marks]

_____

_____

_____

_____

_____

_____

_____

_____

_____

0 2 · 5 Describe the location of an LIC or NEE you have studied.

Name of country _____

[2 marks]

_____

_____

_____

_____

0 2 · 6 Complete the following fact file for the LIC or NEE that you have studied.

[2 marks]

Importance regionally	
Importance internationally	

Mark schemes for the exam papers can be found at **www.oxfordsecondary.com/geog-aqa-answers**.

Study **Figure 5**, two photographs of contrasting examples of economic development in India, which is an NEE.

Figure 5

0 2 · 7   With reference to your case study of an LIC/NEE and **Figure 5**, assess the environmental impacts of economic development.

[6 marks]

_____

_____

_____

_____

_____

_____

_____

_____

_____

_____

_____

Mark schemes for the exam papers can be found at **www.oxfordsecondary.com/geog-aqa-answers**.

Exam practice papers, Paper 2   139

Study **Figure 6**, which gives details of the north–south divide in Great Britain.

Figure 6

Government spending per person

Yorkshire = £7623

E. Midlands = £6983

London = £9176

Life expectancy

Liverpool = 75.7 years

Cambridge = 79.5 years

Southern students are more likely to attend a top university

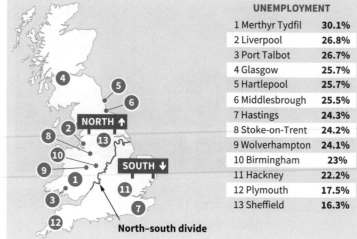

UNEMPLOYMENT	
1 Merthyr Tydfil	**30.1%**
2 Liverpool	**26.8%**
3 Port Talbot	**26.7%**
4 Glasgow	**25.7%**
5 Hartlepool	**25.7%**
6 Middlesbrough	**25.5%**
7 Hastings	**24.3%**
8 Stoke-on-Trent	**24.2%**
9 Wolverhampton	**24.1%**
10 Birmingham	**23%**
11 Hackney	**22.2%**
12 Plymouth	**17.5%**
13 Sheffield	**16.3%**

North–south divide

0 2 · 8 What is the median value for the unemployment blackspots shown on **Figure 6**?

[1 mark]

0 2 · 9 Why may this measure of central tendency give a misleading impression of unemployment in these towns?

[1 mark]

0 2 · 10 Evaluate the strategies that attempt to remove the differences between the north and south of Great Britain.

Use **Figure 6** and your own understanding.

[9 marks]

Continue your answer on a separate sheet of paper

Mark schemes for the exam papers can be found at **www.oxfordsecondary.com/geog-aqa-answers**.

Section C The challenge of resource management

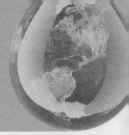

Answer Question 3 (Resources) and **either** Question 4 (Food) **or**
Question 5 (Water) **or** Question 6 (Energy).

Question 3   **Resource management**

Study **Figure 7**, a tweet sent by the National Grid on 21 April 2017.

Figure 7

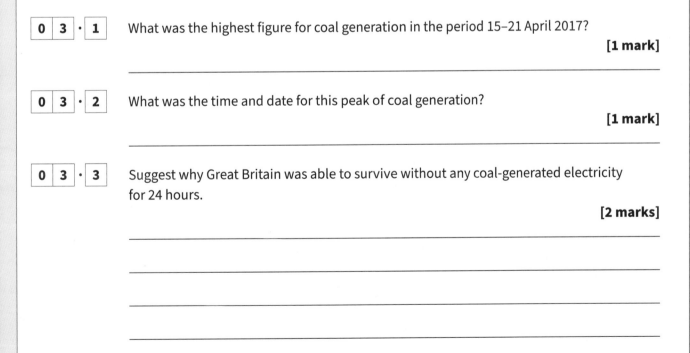

| 0 3 · 1 | What was the highest figure for coal generation in the period 15–21 April 2017? |

[1 mark]

_____

| 0 3 · 2 | What was the time and date for this peak of coal generation? |

[1 mark]

_____

| 0 3 · 3 | Suggest why Great Britain was able to survive without any coal-generated electricity for 24 hours. |

[2 marks]

_____

_____

_____

_____

Mark schemes for the exam papers can be found at **www.oxfordsecondary.com/geog-aqa-answers**.

Exam practice papers, Paper 2   141

Study **Figure 8**, a graph showing how farm sizes changed in the UK between 2005 and 2018.

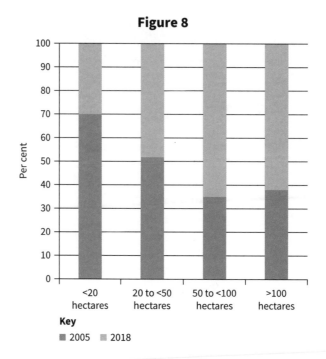

Figure 8

0 3 · 4   What percentage of farms had an area of between 50 and 100 hectares in 2018?

[1 mark]

0 3 · 5   In **Figure 8**, what is the main trend in the size of UK farms between 2005 and 2018?

[1 mark]

0 3 · 6   Suggest how the change in the size of UK farms might affect the provision of food in the UK.

[2 marks]

Mark schemes for the exam papers can be found at **www.oxfordsecondary.com/geog-aqa-answers**.

Study **Figure 9**, which shows areas of water stress in England.

Figure 9

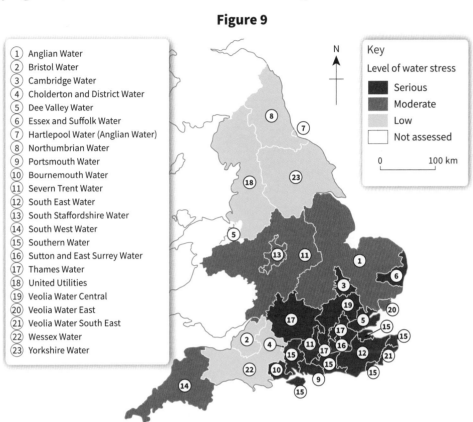

<table>
<tr><td>①</td><td>Anglian Water</td></tr>
<tr><td>②</td><td>Bristol Water</td></tr>
<tr><td>③</td><td>Cambridge Water</td></tr>
<tr><td>④</td><td>Cholderton and District Water</td></tr>
<tr><td>⑤</td><td>Dee Valley Water</td></tr>
<tr><td>⑥</td><td>Essex and Suffolk Water</td></tr>
<tr><td>⑦</td><td>Hartlepool Water (Anglian Water)</td></tr>
<tr><td>⑧</td><td>Northumbrian Water</td></tr>
<tr><td>⑨</td><td>Portsmouth Water</td></tr>
<tr><td>⑩</td><td>Bournemouth Water</td></tr>
<tr><td>⑪</td><td>Severn Trent Water</td></tr>
<tr><td>⑫</td><td>South East Water</td></tr>
<tr><td>⑬</td><td>South Staffordshire Water</td></tr>
<tr><td>⑭</td><td>South West Water</td></tr>
<tr><td>⑮</td><td>Southern Water</td></tr>
<tr><td>⑯</td><td>Sutton and East Surrey Water</td></tr>
<tr><td>⑰</td><td>Thames Water</td></tr>
<tr><td>⑱</td><td>United Utilities</td></tr>
<tr><td>⑲</td><td>Veolia Water Central</td></tr>
<tr><td>⑳</td><td>Veolia Water East</td></tr>
<tr><td>㉑</td><td>Veolia Water South East</td></tr>
<tr><td>㉒</td><td>Wessex Water</td></tr>
<tr><td>㉓</td><td>Yorkshire Water</td></tr>
</table>

Key
Level of water stress
- Serious
- Moderate
- Low
- Not assessed

0   100 km

0 3 · 7   Discuss how water transfer may be needed to maintain supplies across England.
Use **Figure 9** and your own understanding.

[6 marks]

_____

_____

_____

_____

_____

_____

_____

_____

_____

_____

_____

Mark schemes for the exam papers can be found at **www.oxfordsecondary.com/geog-aqa-answers**.

Answer **either** Question 4 (Food) **or** Question 5 (Water) **or** Question 6 (Energy).

Question 4   **Food**

Study **Figure 10**, which gives information about the country of South Sudan in Africa.

Figure 10

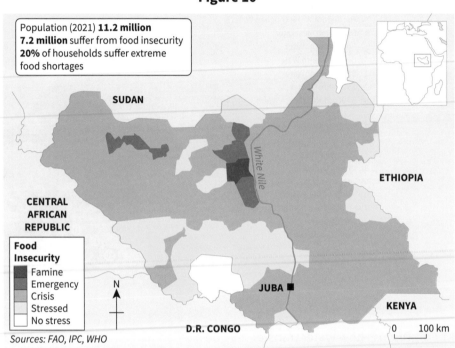

Population (2021) **11.2 million**
7.2 million suffer from food insecurity
20% of households suffer extreme food shortages

SUDAN

CENTRAL
AFRICAN
REPUBLIC

White Nile

ETHIOPIA

**Food
Insecurity**
Famine
Emergency
Crisis
Stressed
No stress

N

JUBA ■

KENYA

D.R. CONGO

0   100 km

Sources: FAO, IPC, WHO

0 4 · 1   What is meant by food insecurity?

[1 mark]

_____

_____

0 4 · 2   Give **two** pieces of evidence from **Figure 10** that show that South Sudan suffers from food insecurity.

[2 marks]

1 _____

2 _____

0 4 · 3   Suggest the impacts of food insecurity on a country.

[2 marks]

_____

_____

_____

_____

Mark schemes for the exam papers can be found at **www.oxfordsecondary.com/geog-aqa-answers**.

0	4	·	4

Choose an example of **either** a large-scale agricultural development **or** a local scheme in an LIC or a NEE that aims to increase the supply of food.

For the example chosen, discuss the extent to which it has been able to increase the supply of food.

Name of example _____

Circle the one you have chosen.

    A large scale agricultural development   A local scheme

[6 marks]

_____

_____

_____

_____

_____

_____

_____

_____

_____

_____

Mark schemes for the exam papers can be found at **www.oxfordsecondary.com/geog-aqa-answers**.

Exam practice papers, Paper 2   **145**

Question 5   Water

Study **Figure 11**, which gives information about the Nile Basin.

Figure 11

While Egypt is entirely dependent on the Nile for its water supply and regards any possible reduction as an issue of national security, some of the world's poorest countries see the river as a vital source for national development.

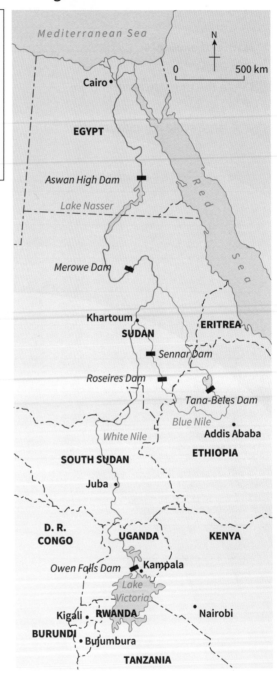

0 5 · 1   What is meant by water insecurity?

[1 mark]

_____

_____

Mark schemes for the exam papers can be found at **www.oxfordsecondary.com/geog-aqa-answers**.

0 5 · 2   Give **two** pieces of evidence from **Figure 11** that show countries in the Nile Basin could suffer from water insecurity.

[2 marks]

1 _____

2 _____

0 5 · 3   Suggest the impacts of water insecurity on a country.

[2 marks]

_____

_____

_____

_____

0 5 · 4   Choose an example of **either** a large-scale water transfer scheme **or** a local scheme in an LIC or NEE, which aims to increase the supply of water.

For the example chosen, discuss the extent to which it has been able to increase the supply of water.

Name of example _____

Circle the one you have chosen.

A large-scale water transfer scheme   A local scheme

[6 marks]

_____

_____

_____

_____

_____

_____

_____

_____

_____

_____

Mark schemes for the exam papers can be found at **www.oxfordsecondary.com/geog-aqa-answers**.

Question 6   **Energy**

Study **Figure 12**, which gives information about the gas supplies in Europe in 2018.

Figure 12

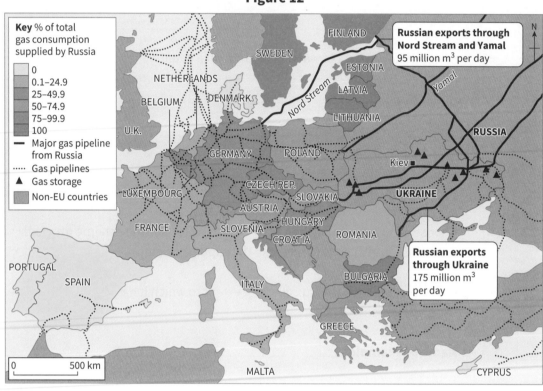

0 6 · 1   What is meant by energy insecurity?

[1 mark]

_____

_____

0 6 · 2   Give **two** pieces of evidence from **Figure 12** that could suggest that Russia's war with Ukraine in 2022 will increase energy insecurity in Europe.

[2 marks]

1 _____

2 _____

Mark schemes for the exam papers can be found at **www.oxfordsecondary.com/geog-aqa-answers**.

0 6 · 3   Suggest the impacts of energy insecurity on a country.

[2 marks]

_____

_____

_____

_____

0 6 · 4   Choose an example of **either** the extraction of a named fossil fuel **or** a local renewable scheme in an LIC or NEE, which aims to increase the supply of energy.

For the example chosen, discuss the extent to which it has been able to increase the supply of energy.

Name of example _____

Circle the one you have chosen.

The use of a named fossil fuel   A local renewable energy scheme

[6 marks]

_____

_____

_____

_____

_____

_____

_____

_____

_____

_____

_____

Mark schemes for the exam papers can be found at **www.oxfordsecondary.com/geog-aqa-answers**.

GCSE 9-1 Geography AQA
Practice Paper

Paper 3 Geographical applications

Time allowed: 1 hour 15 minutes
Total number of marks: 76 (including 6 marks for spelling, punctuation, grammar and specialist terminology [SPaG])

Instructions
Answer **all** questions
Use a clean copy of the pre-release resources booklet

Section A Issue evaluation

Answer **all** questions in this section.

Study **Figure 1** in the resources booklet, 'The tropical rainforest global ecosystem'.

0 1 · 1 Describe the annual rainfall pattern of Belém.

[2 marks]

_____

_____

_____

_____

0 1 · 2 Explain how the global atmospheric system causes the rainfall pattern of Belém.

[2 marks]

_____

_____

_____

_____

0 1 · 3 Explain how climate change can affect nutrient cycling in tropical rainforests.

[2 marks]

_____

_____

_____

_____

Mark schemes for the exam papers can be found at **www.oxfordsecondary.com/geog-aqa-answers**.

| 0 | 1 | · | 4 |

What percentage of the deforestation in Amazonia is caused by cattle ranching?

Shade **one** circle only.

[1 mark]

A   40%   ⬭
B   50%   ⬭
C   60%   ⬭
D   70%   ⬭

| 0 | 1 | · | 5 |

Assess the significance of physical and human factors as being responsible for changing the characteristics of tropical rainforests.

Use **Figure 1** and your own understanding.

[6 marks]

_____

_____

_____

_____

_____

_____

_____

_____

_____

_____

_____

Mark schemes for the exam papers can be found at **www.oxfordsecondary.com/geog-aqa-answers**.

Study **Figure 2** in the resources booklet, 'Biofuels in Indonesia'.

| 0 2 · 1 | Suggest why Indonesia's rainforests have such high levels of biodiversity.

[4 marks]

_____

_____

_____

_____

_____

_____

_____

| 0 2 · 2 | 'The tropical rainforests are important to Indonesia's economy.'

To what extent do you agree with this statement?

[6 marks]

_____

_____

_____

_____

_____

_____

_____

_____

_____

_____

_____

_____

Mark schemes for the exam papers can be found at **www.oxfordsecondary.com/geog-aqa-answers**.

Exam practice papers, Paper 3 153

Study **Figure 3** in the resources booklet, 'The threat to the Indonesian rainforests'.

| 0 | 3 | · | 1 |

What is the link between palm oil production and the changes happening in Indonesian rainforests?

[2 marks]

_____

_____

_____

_____

The following **three** options have been suggested for how Indonesia could manage the country's rainforests in the future.

Option 1	Continue to expand palm oil production to help Indonesia's economy grow as quickly as possible.
Option 2	Slow further expansion of oil palm plantations by taxing palm oil production and monitoring and policing remaining rainforests.
Option 3	Ban palm oil production and create forest reserves, which can only be used for small-scale farming and other sustainable land uses.

| 0 | 3 | · | 2 |

Which of the **three** options do you think will benefit Indonesia without causing long-term damage to the country's rainforests?

Use evidence from the resources booklet and your own understanding to explain why you have reached this decision.

[9 marks]

[+ 3 SPaG marks]

Chosen option _____

_____

_____

_____

_____

_____

_____

_____

_____

_____

Continue your answer on a separate sheet of paper

Mark schemes for the exam papers can be found at **www.oxfordsecondary.com/geog-aqa-answers**.

Section B Fieldwork

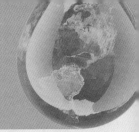

Answer **all** questions in this section.

As part of their investigation of the rural geography in part of the county of Dorset, GCSE students were given a set of secondary data on the facilities in a number of villages in the county.

The data is shown in **Figure 4**.

Figure 4

Village	Population	Church/chapel	Village hall	Primary school	Post office & shop	Food shop	Garage	Bank	Doctor	Pub	Playing field	Cash point	Mobile library	Bus service, daily (D) or weekly (W)
Corfe Castle	980	Yes	1	0	1	2	1	0	1	4	1	1	0	D
East Lulworth	170	Yes	0	0	0	0	0	0	0	1	1	0	1	D
Harmans Cross	340	Yes	1	0	1	0	1	0	0	0	0	1	1	D
Kingston	100	Yes	0	0	0	0	0	0	0	1	0	0	0	W
Langton Maltravers	910	Yes	1	1	1	0	0	0	0	2	1	0	1	D
Ridge	290	No	0	0	0	0	0	0	0	0	0	0	1	W
Steeple	30	Yes	0	0	0	0	0	0	0	0	0	0	0	W
Studland	540	Yes	1	0	1	0	0	0	0	1	1	0	1	D
West Lulworth	770	Yes	1	1	1	0	0	0	0	2	1	1	1	D
Wool	1970	Yes	0	2	1	2	2	0	1	2	1	1	0	D
Worth Maltravers	240	Yes	1	0	1	0	0	0	0	1	0	0	0	D

Date of information: 2006

0 4 · 1   State why this information is an example of secondary data.

[1 mark]

_____

_____

0 4 · 2   What is the modal value for the number of pubs in this survey?

[1 mark]

_____

Mark schemes for the exam papers can be found at **www.oxfordsecondary.com/geog-aqa-answers**.

Resources for Exam 1, Paper 3   155

0 4 · 3 Students carried out a fieldwork enquiry in the same Dorset villages listed in **Figure 4**. **Figure 5** is a scattergraph that shows the link between the number of services and population in each village.

Complete **Figure 5** by plotting the data for Worth Maltravers.

Population **240**, Number of services **3**

[1 mark]

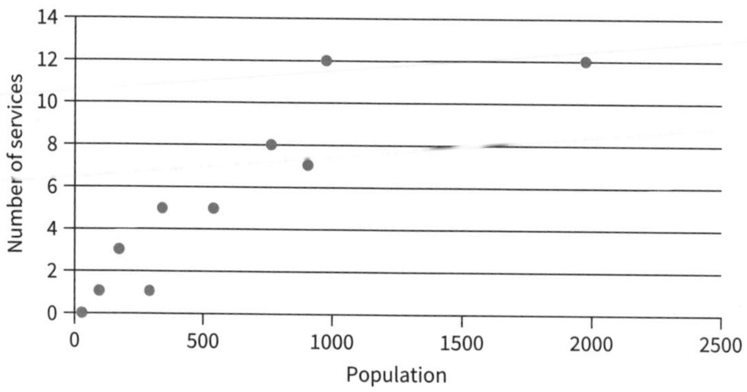

Figure 5

0 4 · 4 Draw in and label the best fit line.

[1 mark]

0 4 · 5 What conclusion could the students make about the hypothesis, 'There is a link between the number of services in a village and its population size'?

[2 marks]

_____

_____

_____

_____

0 4 · 6 Give **two** limitations of this data being used as a basis for a conclusion.

[2 marks]

1 _____

_____

2 _____

_____

Mark schemes for the exam papers can be found at **www.oxfordsecondary.com/geog-aqa-answers**.

156 Exam practice papers, Paper 3

0	4	·	7

As part of their fieldwork enquiry, the students were told to collect some primary data using a sampling technique to add to the secondary data provided.

Suggest **two** possible sampling techniques they could have used.

[2 marks]

1 _____

_____

2 _____

_____

0	4	·	8

Choose **one** of these sampling techniques.

Give **one** advantage and **one** disadvantage of your chosen technique.

[2 marks]

Chosen technique _____

Advantage _____

_____

Disadvantage _____

_____

Study **Figure 6**, a photograph of part of the coast of Northern Ireland, and **Figure 7**, a photograph of the seafront at Brighton in South East England.

Figure 6

Mark schemes for the exam papers can be found at **www.oxfordsecondary.com/geog-aqa-answers**.

Figure 7

0 4 · 9   For **one** of the areas shown in **Figures 6** and **7**, suggest a hypothesis or question that could form the title of a fieldwork enquiry in the area.

[1 mark]

Figure number chosen _____

Hypothesis or question _____

0 4 · 10   For **one** of the areas shown in **Figures 6** and **7**, suggest **one** data collection technique that could be used to test this hypothesis or question in the area.

[1 mark]

Figure number chosen _____

Data collection technique _____

0 4 · 11   Explain why it would be necessary to carry out a risk assessment before carrying out geographical fieldwork in the area you have chosen.

[2 marks]

_____

_____

_____

_____

Mark schemes for the exam papers can be found at **www.oxfordsecondary.com/geog-aqa-answers**.

0 5 · 1 State the title of your **physical** geography fieldwork enquiry.

Title of physical fieldwork enquiry _____

Justify **one** of the data presentation techniques used.

[2 marks]

_____

_____

_____

_____

0 5 · 2 Describe how the timing of when you collected your data could have affected the validity of your results.

[3 marks]

_____

_____

_____

_____

_____

0 5 · 3 State the title of your **human** geography fieldwork enquiry.

Title of human fieldwork enquiry _____

Suggest how your data collection for this enquiry could have been improved to enable your results to be more accurate.

[6 marks]

_____

_____

_____

_____

_____

_____

Mark schemes for the exam papers can be found at **www.oxfordsecondary.com/geog-aqa-answers**.

| 0 | 5 | · | 4 | Assess the extent to which the analysis of the data collected for **either** your human geography enquiry **or** your physical geography enquiry helped your geographical understanding of the topic investigated.

[9 marks]

[+ 3 SPaG marks]

Mark schemes for the exam papers can be found at **www.oxfordsecondary.com/geog-aqa-answers**.

160   **Resources for Exam 1, Paper 3**

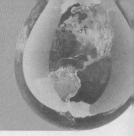

Figure 1

The tropical rainforest global ecosystem

The climate of the tropical rainforests

Belém is a city in the north of Brazil. It lies about 100 km from the Atlantic Ocean on the Amazon River. Belém has a tropical rainforest climate and is subject to the Intertropical Convergence Zone with no cyclones – a true equatorial climate.

The sun is high throughout the year without any definite seasons. Belém's annual average temperature is 32 °C, with over 2900 mm of rainfall and 2200 hours of sunshine each year – an average of 6 hours a day. Humidity remains high and average temperatures only vary a little throughout the year.

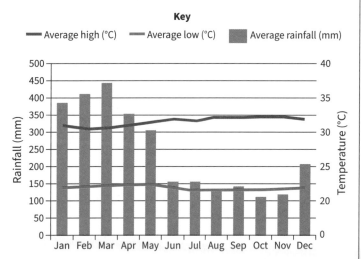

Climate graph for Belém, Brazil

The effect of climate change

A major threat to tropical rainforests is global warming. Rising populations and resource consumption add greenhouse gases to the atmosphere, which causes the climate to change. Some scientists think global warming will lead to species extinction at an unprecedented rate.

During drought conditions, rainforests can increase the effects of climate change because they stop absorbing carbon dioxide and emit it instead. This is because plants stop growing and can therefore no longer absorb the gas. Forest fires are more likely

Impact of global warming on tropical rainforests

Temperature rise	Impact on species	Impact on ecosystem
3 °C	20–50% of species face extinction	<ul><li>Forest gets stressed by drought</li><li>Increased danger of fire</li><li>Flooding causes the loss of mangrove</li><li>Pests and diseases thrive in rising temperatures</li></ul>

in drought conditions, and burning trees release carbon dioxide. Leaf litter dries up, so decomposers die out, which threatens the nutrient cycle. Leaves in the canopy die, reducing the availability of food. This, in turn, affects food webs.

Deforestation adds to the problem. With fewer trees, there is less evaporation and transpiration. This means there are fewer clouds and less rain. This makes droughts more common and more severe.

Mark schemes for the exam papers can be found at **www.oxfordsecondary.com/geog-aqa-answers**.

Figure 1 continued

Causes of deforestation

Farmers in many LICs practise subsistence agriculture, so they have to cut down forest to clear land for growing food and grazing animals. However, research in 2016 showed that the main motive for many farmers in clearing the forest was to grow cash crops. The farmers need the money earned to pay for the rising cost of education and healthcare, and to buy Western goods. It also increases their own status by claiming land as part of their property.

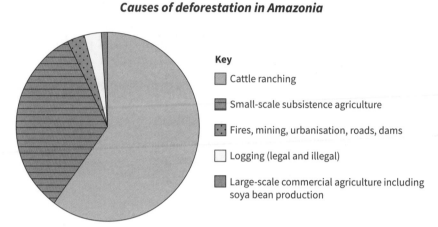

Causes of deforestation in Amazonia

Key
- Cattle ranching
- Small-scale subsistence agriculture
- Fires, mining, urbanisation, roads, dams
- Logging (legal and illegal)
- Large-scale commercial agriculture including soya bean production

Dependence on firewood for fuel contributes to the steady rate of deforestation. The average household in the Congo Basin in Africa uses 1658 kg of firewood a year. A 70 kg bag of charcoal only lasts a family two weeks. The collection of firewood is traditionally carried out by women.

Governments consider rainforests to be a valuable resource. They are keen to cut the forest down for valuable hard woods that they can sell for export. Many of the countries have large debts and see selling cash crops and timber as a way to reduce their debt. This means that, once cleared, forests are converted into other land uses such as pulp, palm and soya plantations, pastures, settlements and hydroelectric power installations. The tropical rainforests contain raw materials such as oil, gas, iron ore and gold. The impact of mining on rainforests is growing due to rising demand and high mineral prices. Mining projects often come with major infrastructure construction, such as roads, railway lines and power stations, putting further pressure on forests and freshwater ecosystems. To reach these resources, forest has to be destroyed.

Forest degradation and the threats from deforestation

Each year, fires burn millions of hectares of forest worldwide. Fires are a part of nature, but degraded forests are particularly vulnerable. The resulting loss has wide-reaching consequences on biodiversity, climate and the economy.

Illegal logging occurs in all types of forests across all continents, destroying nature and wildlife, taking away community livelihoods and distorting trade. Illegally harvested wood reaches markets such as the USA and EU, which encourages the practice. The commercial trade in charcoal also significantly damages forests.

Rates of deforestation in six countries

Country	Average rate of deforestation (%) 2001–19
Malaysia	−15.7
Indonesia	−9.8
Democratic Republic of Congo	−8.0
Brazil	−6.7
Nigeria	6.0
Burundi	−1.2

Mark schemes for the exam papers can be found at **www.oxfordsecondary.com/geog-aqa-answers**.

Figure 2

Biofuels in Indonesia

The issue: biofuels in Indonesia's rainforests

- Indonesia's population and economy have each grown rapidly in recent years.
- Some of Indonesia's economic growth has been based on deforesting tropical rainforests. The cleared land is used to grow palm oil plants.
- Indonesia's government sees this as a way to develop the country. They hope it will lift rural people out of poverty and allow major companies to profit from palm oil.

The location of Indonesia in South-East Asia

Getting to know Indonesia

Indonesia is a large country in Asia. It is spread over numerous large and small islands, with half of all Indonesians living in urban areas. The population was 277.1 million in 2021. The capital Jakarta is located on the island of Java. It has a young population – 26% of the population is aged between 1 and 14 years – and life expectancy is quite high at 72 years. Gross incomes average about $13 436 per person per year as, despite rapid industrialisation, in 2019, 28.5% of the population was still employed in farming.

Indonesian rainforests have a very high level of diversity, but are remote and hard to monitor. Indonesia has more species of mammal than any other nation; an incredible 515 species by most counts. Unfortunately, Indonesia also leads the world in the number of threatened mammals at 135 species – nearly a third of all of its native mammals.

Species group	Percentage of all world species found in Indonesia	Percentage of all world species found in the rest of the world
Plant species	10	90
Mammal species	12	88
Reptiles & amphibians	16	84
Birds	17	83
Fish	25	75

Mark schemes for the exam papers can be found at **www.oxfordsecondary.com/geog-aqa-answers**.

Figure 2 continued

Tropical rainforest in Indonesia

About 10% of the world's remaining tropical rainforest are found in Indonesia, covering 98 million hectares. Yet Indonesia has one of the highest deforestation rates in the world. In the 1960s, about 80% of Indonesia was forested. According to the United Nations, this figure is now down to around 50%. Although the exact figures are not known, it is estimated that more than a million hectares of rainforest are cleared in Indonesia every year.

Rainforest canopy, Kalimantan

Environmental problems

- Many unique species are already extinct and many are endangered, such as the orang-utan.
- Indonesia is the world's third largest emitter of greenhouse gasses, after the USA and China. Most of its emissions are a result of the loss of rainforest (and also peatland). In 2018, Indonesia emitted 1.68% of all global greenhouse gases, more than the combined emissions from the cars, trucks, trains and buses in the USA each year.
- Pesticides used on cleared land pollute waterways and soils.

Social problems

- Burning forests creates smoke that causes problems for air traffic and people's health, which can be affected many hundreds of miles away.

Economic problems

- The 99 million Indonesians who depend on the rainforests for their livelihoods contribute 21% of Indonesia's GDP.
- The livelihoods of the indigenous people who have sustained and been sustained by these forests for centuries are being threatened.

Mark schemes for the exam papers can be found at **www.oxfordsecondary.com/geog-aqa-answers**.

Figure 3

The threat to the Indonesian rainforests

The Indonesian palm oil industry

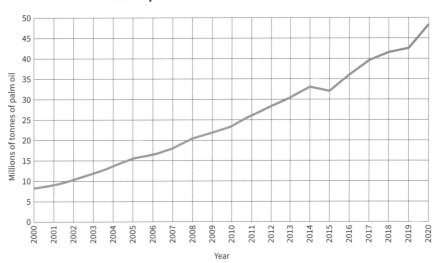

Palm oil production in Indonesia 2000–2020

Indonesia's tropical rainforests are being cleared to create palm oil plantations. The area of oil palm plantations in Indonesia increased from 7.8 million hectares in 2011 to 13 million hectares in 2020.

There is high demand for palm oil from NEEs in Asia, especially India. About 75% of the oil palm plantations are on the islands of Sumatra and Borneo (Kalimantan). About 50% of the plantations are small family-run farms. In total, over 2 million people are employed in the Indonesian palm oil industry. In 2020, palm oil made up 9% of Indonesia's exports, valued at $18 billion. Palm oil is used to make biodiesel (a replacement for diesel made from crude oil), shampoo and lipstick. It can only be grown in tropical areas like Indonesia. Worldwide demand for palm oil has lifted incomes, especially in rural areas.

Why did demand for palm oil increase?
- Palm oil has replaced less healthy, more expensive cooking fats in the West.
- Producers have pushed to keep its price low.
- As Asian countries have grown richer, they have begun to consume more fat, much of it in the form of palm oil.

The EU adopted the Renewable Energy Directive (RED), which included a 10% target for the share of transport fuels coming from biofuels (the most common ingredient being palm oil) by 2020. EU palm oil imports shot up 15% the year after the RED, an all-time high, and 19% the year after that, as biofuel use tripled in the EU between 2011 and 2014. World Bank policies in the 1970s encouraged the Indonesian government to expand palm oil production among small farmers.

Mark schemes for the exam papers can be found at **www.oxfordsecondary.com/geog-aqa-answers**.

Figure 3 continued

Palm oil production in Indonesia 2018 (tons)

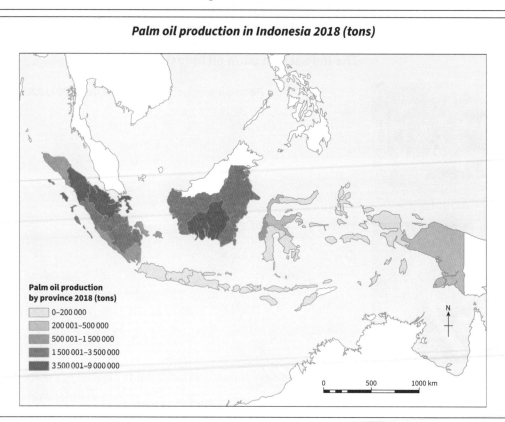

Palm oil production
by province 2018 (tons)
- 0–200 000
- 200 001–500 000
- 500 001–1 500 000
- 1 500 001–3 500 000
- 3 500 001–9 000 000

0   500   1000 km

N

Contrasting views about palm oil development in Indonesia

Organisation	View
WWF is an environmental pressure group and NGO.	'Large areas of tropical forests have been cleared to make room for vast oil palm plantations – destroying habitats for many endangered species, including rhinos, elephants and tigers. In some cases, the expansion of plantations has led to the eviction of forest-dwelling people.' – *From the WWF article 'Environmental and Social Impacts of Palm Oil Production' at wwf.panda.org*
World Growth is a pressure group that promotes globalisation.	'Palm oil provides developing nations and the poor with a path out of poverty. Expanding sustainable agriculture such as oil palm plantations provides plantation owners and their workers with a means to improve their standard of living.' – *From the World Growth report 'The Economic Benefit of Palm Oil to Indonesia', Feb 2011*
Cargill is a TNC based in the USA that grows, processes and sells palm oil.	'Millions of people around the world depend on palm oil. We believe that palm oil should be produced sustainably. We have made a commitment that the palm oil products we supply will be certified as coming from sustainable forests by 2020.' – *Adapted from various Cargill policies on palm oil at www.cargill.com*

Mark schemes for the exam papers can be found at **www.oxfordsecondary.com/geog-aqa-answers**.

Answer guidance

Pages 6–13

Activity 1
Your own answer.

Activity 2
Your own answer.

Activity 3
State: Provide a simple statement

Calculate: Work out something

Suggest: Use evidence to identify possible ideas or outcomes

To what extent: Judge the importance of an outcome or decision

Explain: Give reasons/say why

Describe: Write what you can see

Activity 4
First row: ✗ No direct reference is made to the photo

Last row: ✓ Clear sequence in the formation of the waterfall

Activity 5
(a) 'Figure 2 shows that…'

(b) 'Pacific Ocean', 'Japan', 'the Philippines', etc.

(c) 'there are some anomalies with isolated volcanoes in parts of Asia and Africa'

Activity 6
(a)–(c)

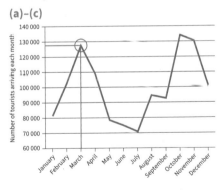

(d) March; 130 000; 70 000; September

Activity 7
(a) Foreground of photo

(b) Background of photo

Activity 8
Figure 5 shows the location of megacities in the world in 2030. Megacities are located all over the world. They are concentrated particularly in Asia, for example in India and China. There are lots of megacities in China. There are few megacities in Africa – only three. Elsewhere, there are some megacities in Europe and in North and South America. A lot of megacities are located on the coast. This is because they are ports and have developed as trading centres. So, as the map shows, there are lots of megacities all over the world.

Activity 9
(a) The student didn't state the size in per cent. The answer should be '80%'.

(b) • 'about 7%' should be 'about 14%' – the student misread the axis.

• 'secondary and primary sectors' should be 'secondary and tertiary sectors'.

• '64%' should be '43%' – the student misread the graph, looking at Brazil by mistake.

Pages 14–15

Activity 1
(a) Possible answers: About 6300 people killed **S**; 600 000 people displaced **S**; Power lines and crops destroyed **Ec**; Tacloban airport terminal badly damaged **Ec**; 6 million people lost their source of income **Ec**; Looting and violence broke out **S**; Coast strewn with debris **En**; Shortages of food and water led to outbreaks of disease **S**; Water sources polluted by seawater and sewage **En**; Many hospitals, schools and shops destroyed **S**.

(b) **Economic:** Blocked roads and landslides would have made it difficult to transport goods. This would have affected local businesses.

Environmental: Flooding would have inundated normally dry environments. Habitats may have been damaged and animals killed or forced to migrate.

Activity 2
(a) • Open green spaces make this a pleasant place to work. **En**

• Land on the edge of Cambridge is cheaper than in the centre. **Ec**

• There is good road access for the transport of people, goods and services. **Ec**

• There are opportunities (grass, paths) for recreation and fitness. **S**

• Nearby housing provides homes for workers. **S**

• Low-rise, high-tech buildings produce low levels of carbon emissions (lack of chimneys). **En**

(b) There are several options for each label.

Now try this!

• Economic advantages could include references to nearby roads, facilitating transportation of workers, goods and services; several companies on the same site can benefit economically from each other (cost sharing, etc.); relatively cheap land on the edge of the city.

• Environmental advantages could include an attractive site (trees and grassy areas) for people to work; retention (and creation?) of diverse natural habitats (grass, trees, etc.) promoting species diversity; a low environmental impact (air pollution) with the lack of heavy industrial processes (no chimneys).

• You must refer to evidence from Figure 1.

• You can only achieve Level 1 if you refer to **either** economic advantages **or** environmental advantages. To achieve Level 2 (4 marks), you must refer to both.

Pages 16–17

Activity 1
(a) • Freshwater pond **L**

• Sahara Desert **R**

• Town centre **L**

• Middle East **R**

• China **N**

• Climate change **G**

(b) • Local examples: retail park, woodland, river, etc.

• Regional examples: Prairies (North America), Thar Desert, etc.

• Global examples: world's oceans, tundra, etc.

Activity 2

Short-term effects	Long-term effects
• Buildings collapse • People are killed or injured • Electricity is cut off • People need water, food, shelter and medicine	• Damage to businesses result in falling incomes • Children's education suffers if schools destroyed • Some people migrate to safer areas • Poor conditions may lead to disease

Now try this!

- To achieve a Level 2 mark, you need to refer to evidence in the photo (e.g. damage to electricity lines and houses) when identifying immediate responses.
- Immediate responses might include search and rescue, and providing water, food and shelter.

Pages 18–19

Activity 1

(a) More job opportunities **S (could be Ec if linked to wages)**

(b) Improved services (healthcare and education) **S**

(c) Increased incomes **Ec**

(d) Increased food supply **S**

(e) Trees planted **En**

(f) Ecosystems preserved **En**

(g) Less migration away from the area **S**

(h) Tourism brings money into the area **Ec**

Activity 2

Possible labels might include:

- Extensive green area for food production, carbon absorption, recreation, etc.
- Wind turbines and windmill for renewable wind energy.
- Planting of trees (absorption of carbon dioxide, giving shade, protection of habitats, etc.).
- Water body to moderate the climate, provide water storage to prevent flooding, possible water supply, recreation.

Now try this!

- Select only **one** from food, water or energy.
- Make sure that you explain (give reasons).
- You need to write about at least

two strategies (e.g. for water: water conservation/groundwater management/recycling/grey water).

- For each strategy, state explicitly how it ensures sustainable supplies for the future (i.e. why it is long-lasting and doesn't harm the environment).

Pages 20–21

Activity 1

Investment: China has invested billions of dollars in Africa, helping to build new roads, bridges and sports stadiums; the headquarters of the African Union were paid for by China; China has paid for a power plant in Zimbabwe and hydroelectric power in Madagascar.

Tourism: Money generated can be spent on transport, health and education; tourism brings employment opportunities and increases incomes.

Aid: Local aid projects provide health centres and improvements to services, such as water; Goat Aid provides goats in Malawi, improving diets and source of income (milk, cheese, etc.); the UK provides aid to Pakistan, Ethiopia and Bangladesh.

Activity 2

(a)–(c) See the graph below.

(d) LICs have high levels of poverty. People have limited access to healthcare, food and safe water. As a result, death rates can be high (especially for the young and old). High infant mortality, limited acceptance of contraception, and the need to have large families to work on the land result in high birth rates.

Activity 3

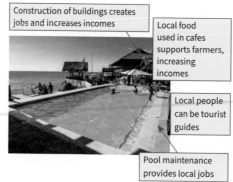

Construction of buildings creates jobs and increases incomes

Local food used in cafes supports farmers, increasing incomes

Local people can be tourist guides

Pool maintenance provides local jobs

Now try this!

- Refer specifically to evidence in the photo.
- Use your labels (Activity 3) and make clear links between tourism and reductions in the development gap.
- For example, tourism provides opportunities for employment in construction and maintenance, as well as in hotels and restaurants. Local people benefit by having higher incomes and the government receives tax income. This will help to reduce the development gap between the rich and the poor.

Pages 22–23

Activity 1

Causes	Effects
Earthquake	Tsunami
Volcanic eruption	Emissions of greenhouse gases
Deforestation	Loss of natural habitat
Overgrazing in hot deserts	Desertification
Rapid urbanisation	Squatter settlements
Aid	Reduction of the development gap
Economic development	Improved quality of life

Activity 2

(a) Explain how plants and animals have adapted to the conditions in a hot desert (or cold environment).

(b) Explain how hard engineering structures can reduce the impacts of river flooding.

(c) Explain how urban regeneration can help to solve problems in urban areas.

Activity 3

(a) True

(b) By decomposition

(c) Labels linked to the climate are: 'Gain from precipitation', 'Loss by runoff' (rainfall), 'Loss by leaching' (rainfall), 'Gain from weathering'.

(d) Biomass will be reduced significantly. This will reduce the 'uptake by plants' transfer. 'Falling leaves, twigs and branches' may increase during deforestation but will then decrease. This will impact on the 'Decomposition by bacteria and fungi' transfer too. Other transfers may change. Litter and soil may increase slightly due to changes in the transfers.

Pages 24–25

Activity 1

(a) Top diagram = constructive plate margin. Middle diagram = destructive plate margin. Bottom diagram = conservative plate margin.

(b) Label the volcano in the top diagram, and the volcano in the middle diagram. (There is no volcano in the bottom diagram.)

(c) Pressure builds up at plate margins due to the movement of the plates. This pressure is released as sudden jerks, causing rocks to fracture and triggering earthquakes (ground shaking).

(d) Magma rises to the ground surface to form volcanoes.

(e) There is no magma present.

Activity 2

Missing words are: solar; Earth; greenhouse; carbon; space; deforestation*; transport*; effect; temperature

(*Possible answers; others are acceptable.)

Now try this!

Answers could include deforestation, an increase in vehicles, more intensive farming, etc. A clear link needs to be made between human activity and an increase in carbon dioxide in the atmosphere.

Pages 26–27

Activity 1

Labels should point to the following:
(a) Cloud
(b) Ground
(c) Leaves of tree/flowers
(d) Rabbit
(e) Fox
(f) Worms/insects/fungi

Activity 2

(a) A food web is a diagram showing how plants and animals rely upon each other for food.

(b) Examples include agoutis and butterflies.

(c) Agoutis are herbivores, eating plants. These plants will thrive and may start to dominate others in the ecosystem. Jaguars will eat more alternative animals, such as tapirs, which could reduce their numbers and affect the ecosystem.

Activity 3

(a) With fire (burning).

(b) The land is blackened, with the remains of tree stumps. Grass is the only vegetation.

(c)

> Reduction in variety of plants/trees, destroying habitats and reducing biodiversity.

> Fire may kill some animals or drive them away from the area.

> Grasses dominate the ground, restricting biodiversity.

Now try this!

Two causes only from Figure 4 to be identified and described briefly. There must be clear links between the cause and the loss of biodiversity. Examples might include:

- Conversion of land for palm oil production in Indonesia, affecting the habitats of wildlife and reducing biodiversity.

- Mining causes deforestation, destroying habitats and polluting water supplies, reducing biodiversity.

Pages 28–29

Activity 1

Coastal/river landscapes	
Process	**Definition**
Hydraulic action (power)	The power of water erodes the cliff or bed and banks of a river
Abrasion	Rocks carried by the sea or in a river are used to carry out erosion
Attrition	Rocks smash together and break into smaller and smoother particles
Solution	Erosion: dissolving of rocks or minerals Transportation: transport of dissolved chemicals in the water
Traction	Material is rolled along the sea/river bed

Glacial landscapes	
Process	**Definition**
Freeze-thaw weathering	Repeated cycles of freezing and thawing, enlarging cracks and causing rocks to break away
Abrasion	Rocks carried beneath a glacier grind away the underlying bedrock (like sandpaper)
Plucking	Loose rocks are 'plucked' from solid bedrock as meltwater freezes them to the base of a glacier
Rotational slip	Slippage of ice along a curved surface
Bulldozing	The snout of an advancing glacier pushes deposited sediment

Activity 2

From left to right: 2, 4, 1, 3

Activity 3

(a) 1 Afforestation/tree planting; 2 Channel straightening; 3 dam and reservoir

(b) 1 soft; 2 hard; 3 hard

(c) 1 Intercepts rainfall and slows transfer of water to the river; 2 Speeds up water flow through a vulnerable area; 3 Stores water and regulates its flow downstream preventing flooding

Pages 30–31

Activity 1

See the map below.

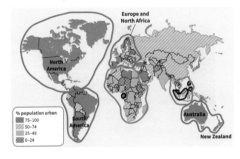

Activity 2

(a) Plot the value for 2030 accurately at 17.6 m and join it with a dotted line to the value for 2020.

(b) 12.5 – 3.1 = 9.4

(c) Slow and steady growth between 1950 and 1990, from 1 m to 3.1 m (2.1 m in 40 years).

(d) Rapid growth since 1990 (3.1 m) to 17.6 m in 2030 (14.5 m in 40 years). The graph suggests a slight reduction in growth from 2020 to 2030.

(e) The global and national rankings suggest that Guangzhou's growth is outstripping other cities. Globally, Guangzhou is ranked 71st in 1950 and 16th in 2030. Nationally, Guangzhou rises from 7th to 4th in the same time period.

Activity 3

Labels might identify green spaces with trees, pedestrian areas and walkways, no cars allowed, extensive use of glass in buildings, open-sided buildings (to allow air to flow, cutting costs of air conditioning), etc.

Pages 32–33

Activity 1

(a) Supply industries supply larger industries with component parts (e.g. tyres for cars).

(b) employment/services/water/ healthcare/educated/healthier/ shops/community facilities

(c) From one stage to the next, the economic growth multiplies. So, for example, the opening of one factory may support 10 smaller factories supplying components.

Activity 2

From top to bottom: 3, 4, 1, 5, 2

Activity 3

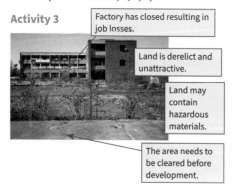

Factory has closed resulting in job losses.

Land is derelict and unattractive.

Land may contain hazardous materials.

The area needs to be cleared before development.

Now try this!

- The photo of a derelict industrial building suggests that people have lost their jobs. This will affect incomes and may have other knock-on effects (less income for shops and services).

- Factory closure may affect other industries in the supply chain, resulting in loss of orders (income), which may lead to further closures and unemployment.

- The photo shows a depressed and derelict area, which may negatively affect house prices and lower the status of the area.

- Your own understanding might involve the multiplier effect (in reverse) leading to a spiral of decline.

- Good answers may refer to scale – local scale as indicated by the photo together with regional and national scale, as supply industries are affected and tax income reduced (and government support expenditure increased).

Pages 34–35

Activity 1

(a) Brown/red.

(b)–(c) See the map below.

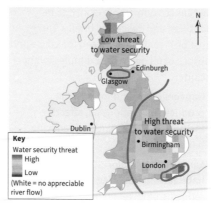

Low threat to water security

Edinburgh

Glasgow

High threat to water security

Birmingham

Dublin

London

Key
Water security threat
High
Low
(White = no appreciable river flow)

(d) In the UK, there is a South East/ North West split in water security. In the South East there is a high level of threat whereas in the North West there is a low level of threat. The highest levels of threat are in the far South East (Kent/Sussex). The lowest levels of threat are in the Scottish Highlands. One anomaly is the central lowlands of Scotland (Glasgow to Edinburgh) where there is a high level of threat.

Activity 2

(a) • Commercial food production and food processing raises tax money for the government. **Ec**

- Most people are well fed and able to lead healthy lives. **S**

- Obesity has become a significant problem among children. **S**

- Exporting surplus food provides money for the government. **Ec**

(b) Obesity has become a significant problem among children.

Activity 3

(a) Draw a horizontal line to divide the map into roughly equal halves.

(b) True

(c) False

(d) The Sahara Desert is situated in North Africa.

Pages 36–37

Now try this!

1. B

2. D

3. D

Pages 38–39

Now try this!

1.1 Graph should show an incline from 0 to 900 m for tropical rainforest and again from 900 to 1800 m for temperate forest. Both should be done for 1 mark – no marks if only one completed correctly.

1.2 Coniferous forest exists between 1800 and 3800 m.

   1 mark for both figures correct. Allow a range of 3600–3900 m for the second figure.

1.3 Allow a range between 4600 and 4900 m. Answer does not need to say 'above sea level'.

2.1 B

2.2 North-east. No other answer is acceptable.

2.3 Accept between 4.25 and 4.75 km.

Pages 40–41

Now try this!

1. 1 mark for any one of the following:

   Formed in layers/layered; formed from river deposits/sea or coastal deposits/glacial; deposits/wind-blown deposits; any other correct characteristic

2. 1 mark for any one of the following:

   Freeze-thaw ('frost shattering'); breakdown by plant roots

3. 1 mark for any one of the following:

   General land uses, e.g. industry, housing, forestry; specific activities, e.g. mining, factories, hotels, office blocks

   Activities must be linked to the landscape, e.g. fishing is incorrect.

4. 1 mark for any one of the following:

   Changes in Earth's orbit/Milankovitch cycles; variations in heat output from the sun/sunspots; volcanic activity

5. 1 mark for any one of the following:

   Past ice ages/glacial periods; the Little Ice Age; past volcanic eruptions, e.g. Mount Tambora

6. Must be a positive answer, for example:

   Where more people leave a city to live elsewhere than are entering it; population movement has more people leaving than arriving

   These answers would not be acceptable:

   People leaving a city; fewer people are coming to live in a city

7. Human Development Index (all three words must be correct)

8. 1 mark for any one of the following:

   Land occupied by a cluster of businesses; business areas located on the edge of a city/town; a recent estate containing retail and workplaces; an area of modern industries/offices where companies may get grants for moving there

9. 1 mark for any one of the following:

   People may be killed/injured; homes may be damaged/destroyed; loss of power supplies/water; any answer which implies direct damage caused by the tectonic event itself

10. A resource which: is infinite/comes from natural sources such as wind or sun/will never run out

11. The wearing away of the landscape

Pages 42–43

Now try this!

1. Allow 1 mark for the way given and 1 mark for developed explanation, e.g.:
   - *There are many slum areas consisting of poor quality housing (1), which means that health may be poor. (1)*
   - *Some people are very wealthy and have a high quality of life (1), so that there is huge inequality in the city. (1)*

2. 1 mark for the feature and 1 mark for developed descriptive point, e.g.:
   - *The fastest winds circulate around the storm (1) with very low pressure air. (1)*

   - *The centre of the storm is calm (1) with calm conditions and clear skies. (1)*

3. 1 mark for the measure and 1 mark for explanation of how it measures development.
   - Examples of the measure include GDP, GNI, HDI (HDI is allowable since it incorporates GNI). No marks for a social indicator, e.g. literacy rates.
   - Explanations could include: GDP/GNI because it measures the wealth produced by a country in a year.

4. 1 mark for the way given and 1 mark for developed explanation, e.g.:

   There could be investment in industries/factories (1), so that there are more jobs for people. (1)

Pages 44–45

Activity 1

Answer 1: 1 mark – no development, so no second mark

Answer 2: 2 marks – rising sea level (1), 'large range' (1)

Answer 3: 0 marks – 'changing' is not the same as 'rising', and 'ice caps are melting' is an explanation, not description

Answer 4: 2 marks – 'increases have a wide range' (1) and use of data to illustrate (1)

Now try this!

1. 1 mark for the feature and 1 mark for developed descriptive point, e.g.: *Cloud circulating (1) in an anti-clockwise direction. (1)*

2. 1 mark for a difference and 1 mark for developed point (e.g. by quoting data), e.g.: *More people live further from work in a megacity (1), e.g. only half are within 15 minutes of work compared to 82% in the rest of the country. (1)*

Pages 46–47

Now try this!

1. 1 mark for the feature described and 1 mark for a developed point, e.g.:
   - *Set up seismometers (1), so that earth tremors before an eruption can be detected. (1)*
   - *Develop evacuation plans (1), so that people know where to go if there's an eruption. (1)*

2. 1 mark for the cause and 1 mark for developed explanation, e.g.:
   - *Houses may not be well built (1), so that strong winds cause them to collapse. (1)*
   - *Water taps or wells may be destroyed (1), so that people lose their water supply. (1)*

3. 1 mark for the feature and 1 mark for a developed point, e.g.:
   - *Plates pull apart (1), so that magma rises to the surface as lava. (1)*
   - *Lava erupts out of the crack (1), so that volcanoes form there. (1)*

4. 1 mark for the transport feature described and 1 mark for a developed point, e.g.:
   - *UK cities can set up congestion charging (1), so that people find it cheaper to use public transport. (1)*
   - *UK cities can use hydrogen buses (1), so that CO_2 emissions are reduced. (1)*

Pages 48–49

Now try this!

1. 1 mark for the feature and 1 mark for a developed point, e.g.:
   - *Setting up weather satellites (1), so that people can predict when a tropical cyclone might arrive. (1)*
   - *Building shelters (1) to give people somewhere safe to go if a tropical cyclone arrives. (1)*

2. 1 mark for the feature and 1 mark for a developed point, e.g.:
   - *Setting up weather satellites (1) to track a tropical cyclone and forecast its arrival. (1)*
   - *Building raised shelters (1), which are designed to be above any floods and protect people. (1)*

3. 1 mark for the feature and 1 mark for a developed description, e.g.:
   - *Trees have buttress roots (1), which spread outwards from the tree. (1)*
   - *Leaves have pointed tips (1), so that water can run off easily. (1)*

4. 1 mark for the feature and 1 mark for a developed description, e.g.:
   - *Trees have buttress roots (1), which support the weight of the tree. (1)*
   - *Tall, emergent trees grow high above the rest (1), which allows them to compete for light. (1)*

Answer guidance

Pages 50–51

Now try this!

1. 1 mark for a feature and 2 marks for a developed explanation of the difference, e.g.: *Volcanoes at constructive boundaries are gently sloping (1), whereas those at destructive boundaries are steeply sloping (1) because of the differences in lava temperatures. (1)*

2. 1 mark for each of a sequence of changes brought by a change of land use, e.g.: *Changing from farmland to urban land removes permeable soil (1) and replaces it with impermeable concrete or tarmac (1), which means that surface runoff is much faster. (1)*

3. 1 mark for an impact and 2 marks for a developed explanation of the difference, e.g.: *Economic development leads to an increase in urbanisation (1) because there is more employment in urban areas (1) as industrialisation leads to greater numbers of factories. (1)*

Pages 52–53

Now try this!

1.1 28.25 °C (units are not needed)

1.2 12 °C (units are not needed)

1.3 345.4 (answer must be exact)

1.4 87.6% (1). Working should show amount fallen in rainy season June–Sept as 302.5, divided by the total and multiplied by 100. (1)

2.1 7.5 times (1)

2.2 52 billion (must say 'billion' to gain the mark)

Pages 54–55

Now try this!

1.1 Median Y, Lower quartile Z, Upper quartile X

1.2 68 (1); 49 (1)

Pages 56–64

Activity 1

(a) • Buildings may be very poorly built.
- People have little money so may have little chance to recover.

(b) • Photo: houses have collapsed.
- Own understanding: GDP is low.

(c) • Photo: building materials look weak and poor quality.
- Own understanding: low GDP means there are few recovery or rescue services.

Activity 2

Refer to the annotations in the Worked example on page 59.

Activity 3

This answer gets 2 marks.

'Wooden shacks like the one in the photo ...' (1), and 'so that they would fall down' (1). The second part of the answer is not relevant.

Activity 4

Evidence: One strength and one weakness required.

Command word: 'Explain' means give reasons for the strength and weakness.

Focus: The question is about one indicator of development shown in Figure 1, not all three.

What you have to write: One strength and one weakness of chosen indicator of development and a reason for each.

Activity 5

(a) • HDI has advantages.
- HDI has disadvantages.

(b) • Advantage: HDI includes data about a country's literacy and life expectancy.
- Disadvantage: Some people may be much healthier and better educated than this.

(c) • An advantage of HDI is that it gives a good idea of the social development of a country.
- A disadvantage of HDI is that it is a blanket figure for the whole country and different parts of the country may vary.

Activity 6

You should write: 1) an advantage of your chosen indicator; 2) what your chosen indicator measures; 3) why this is an advantage. Repeat for a disadvantage, e.g.:

- Death rate – an advantage is that it is a good measure of a country's health services; a disadvantage is that some places in that country might be much worse or much better than that.

- Percentage of population with access to safe water – this is a good measure because water and how clean it is can determine a nation's health. A disadvantage is that it's a general figure, and rural areas are often worse than cities for safe water supply.

Activity 7

Make sure you compare your answer with the guidance given. Have you included an advantage and disadvantage, and reasons why it is like this?

Activity 8

This answer gets to the top of Level 2 and 4 marks because the candidate has:

- stated clearly what is meant by HDI and how it is measured
- explained its advantage in combining three measures of development in a single figure
- explained two advantages of HDI – how it is calculated, and why it does not work in countries such as Saudi Arabia
- quoted evidence from the table of data in explaining the points above.

Activity 9

- Briefly explain the link between health and death rate.
- Explain one disadvantage of death rate, e.g. that it might not tell you about health improvements such as vaccinations that will reduce death rate.

Now try this!

Your answer should include:

- Use of Figure 1 – showing the relationship between headlands (including their names) and areas of hard rock type (limestone/chalk); the relationship between bays (including their names) and areas of softer rock type (clays and sands).

- Your understanding – explaining how softer rocks would be eroded more than harder rocks.

Pages 65–67

Activity 1

(a) You should make sure that the four boxes, when read out in order, form a sequence, e.g.:
Box 2: *... which increases beach size and protects the local cliffs ...* **Box 3:** *... but that means less sand will be transported further along the coast*

Box 4: … *and therefore cliff erosion rates will increase there as waves will erode the cliffs more easily.*

(b) Examples could include:

Level 2

1: Names a method of hard engineering and explains what it is intended to do.

2: Explains the sequence of processes that lead to problems elsewhere.

Level 1

3: Names a method of hard engineering but may not explain what it is intended to do.

4: Explains some processes but these are not sequenced or linked to problems elsewhere.

Activity 2

This answer is Level 2. It shows a clear understanding of coastal groynes and their purpose in preventing longshore drift. It applies the situation well by explaining a sequence of the processes leading to problems further along the coast. It is worth 4 marks.

Activity 3

Your answer should:

- include a single change of land use, e.g. from forest to farmland or from farmland to housing or urban development
- explain how this leads to a change of surface, e.g. from permeable soil to impermeable concrete
- show how this affects the hydrological cycle, e.g. removing the interception zone or altering infiltration rates, such as water passing quickly through drains in a town
- explain the effects on rivers and how this leads to flooding.

Activity 4

(a) Examples could include:

Level 2:

1: Names a change of land use and can explain its effects on the hydrological cycle.

2: Explains the sequence of processes that lead to greater flood risk along a river.

Level 1:

3: Names a change of land use but its effects on the hydrological cycle are not clear.

4: Explains some processes but these are not sequenced or linked to how flood risk is increased.

(b) Your own answer.

Pages 68–71

Now try this!

1. Your answer should:
   - include references to both derelict land and deprived areas of Glasgow
   - suggest reasons for derelict land, e.g. closed industries/deindustrialisation
   - suggest reasons for the deprivation found in the same areas of the city, e.g. loss of jobs when industries closed.

   You must refer to at least one piece of evidence on the map, Figure 1.

2. Your answer should include:
   - one impact of urban growth, e.g. increased rural–urban migration, or rapid increase in the urban population
   - an explanation of how this has affected quality of life, e.g. insufficient housing
   - an extension of the explanation, e.g. people may set up slum housing built of cheap materials close to the railways line where it is unsafe
   - reference to at least one feature of the photograph in Figure 2.

3. Your answer should include:
   - reference to Figure 3 (Figure 3 shows a reduction in Arctic sea ice by 50% compared to the 1979–2000 average) and also to your own understanding
   - clear connections between the evidence and climate change
   - other evidence (your own understanding) such as long-term records from the study of ice cores, shrinking glaciers, rises in sea level and changes in seasons, as indicated by plants flowering early or changes in bird migration.

Activity

Your own comments.

Pages 72–75

Activity 1

(a) • A spit is formed from deposition and from river flow.
   • A sand bar/tombolo also results from deposition.

(b) • Photo: there is a spit in the photo.
   • Own understanding: explanation of longshore drift.

(c) • Photo: how drift towards the photo has led to the development of a spit, also shaped into a hook by the river.
   • Own understanding: explanation of swash and backwash and net gain of material over time forming the spit.

(d) • Photo: both the river and the sea have been important.
   • Own understanding: a sand bar is created where there is only deposition from the sea – there is no river to affect the shape; mud flats build up in the still water behind the spit.

Activity 2

Refer to the annotations in the Worked example on page 75.

Pages 76–80

Activity 1

Evidence: Need two impacts – one from own knowledge, and one from the photo.

Command word: 'Suggest' means give impacts that look reasonable based on what is in the photo.

Focus: The question is about rainforest clearance, so need to suggest two impacts based on what is in the photo and own knowledge.

What you have to write: Two impacts for 4 marks, and a reason for each one.

Activity 2

(a) • Photo: deforestation has destroyed the tree cover.
   • Own understanding: rainforest soils are very infertile without the forest cover.

(b) Evidence:
   • Photo: the soil is now exposed to heavy rain.
   • Own understanding: there is ash on the surface from where the forest has been burned.

(c) • Photo: the exposed soil would erode quickly without any protection.
   • Own understanding: the ash would be fertile but it would not last long if rains eroded it.

(d) • Photo: the impacts on soil erosion would be great.
   • Own understanding: there would be no fertility left in the soil.

Answer guidance

Activity 3

Your answer should include:

- one impact of rainforest clearance that you know about, e.g. low soil fertility, soil erosion in rainforest areas
- one impact of rainforest clearance from the photo, e.g. exposed soil
- explanation of the impacts of each of these, e.g. rapid soil erosion, lower soil fertility
- reference to at least one feature of the photograph in Figure 1.

Activity 4

Your own comments.

Activity 5

This candidate just gets a Level 2. The strengths of this answer are:

The candidate knows some impacts of rainforest clearance but it is generalised, for example, there is little terminology (e.g. 'soil erosion') ('Point'). The candidate refers directly to the photo ('Evidence'). The two explanations show that the candidate knows the consequences of clearing rainforest ('Explanation').

By partly meeting the criteria for Level 2, the answer is lower Level 2 and earns 3 marks.

Now try this!

Your answer should include the following:

- Two paragraphs, which are about the evidence to suggest why people might disagree with the statement. The paragraphs should be different, e.g. one might be about social concerns such as poor housing, while another might deal with health issues.
- Named examples of urban problems from specific cities (e.g. Rio) or named communities (e.g. Rocinha).
- Evidence which supports your case with explanations of how particular problems have developed, e.g. why housing is so poor.

Pages 81–84

Activity 1

Evidence: Need 2 or 3 impacts from a major UK city – at least one impact from own understanding, and at least one from the map.

Command word: 'Discuss' means give a range of examples (for 6 marks, that means 2 or 3 examples), from both the map and also from own understanding.

Focus: The question is about international migration in a major UK city – need to suggest at least one impact based on the map and at least one from own knowledge.

What you have to write: Need 2 or 3 impacts for 6 marks, and a developed reason for each. Name the city.

Activity 2

(a) • Map: Asian-British people are concentrated in certain areas.
- Own understanding: different migrant communities live in different areas of cities.

(b) • Map: this includes areas like Southall or Hounslow.
- Own understanding: most cities have areas where there are mosques or ethnic shopping areas.

(c) • Map: this is probably where there is work available.
- Own understanding: this is for the community to buy particular foods or follow their religions.

(d) • Map: it gives support to people if they live close together.
- Own understanding: ethnic areas like these make big impacts on changing the look of cities.

Activity 3

Your answer should include:

- 1 or 2 impacts of international migration that you know about, e.g. the ways in which ethnic communities change the appearance of cities
- 1 or 2 impacts of international migration from the map, e.g. named areas where Asian British people live in London
- explanations of these impacts on a named major city, e.g. ways in which different migrant groups live in different parts of cities such as London
- reference to at least one feature of the map in Figure 1.

Activity 4

Your own comments.

Activity 5

The criteria for Level 3 apply to this answer because the candidate has:

- mentioned both the reasons for growth and the changing character of Bristol
- named a specific country for immigrants, and there is an example of the kind of cultural events that have resulted from immigration. It does not matter that these examples are chosen from different cities, as long as they are large and in the UK.

The candidate's interpretation of the map about the impacts of international migration is not so strong. Although the candidate refers to Figure 1, there is no real interpretation of what it shows. By meeting the first Level 3 descriptor fully, and the second one partly, the answer is low Level 3 in quality, so is worth 5 marks.

Pages 85–91

Activity 1

(a) • Global climate is warming.
- Sea levels are rising.
- The evidence for climate change is overwhelming.

(b) • Global temperatures are 1 °C warmer than in the early 20th century.
- Sea levels have risen by about 200 mm in the past century.
- The evidence includes retreating glaciers from all over the world.

(c) • Greenhouse gas emissions have increased.
- This has caused greater flooding globally – it's not just flooding in one place.
- The glaciers have been measured and photographed over more than a century.

(d) • The evidence is reliable because there are more recording stations now, all saying the same thing.
- The evidence is reliable because sea level rise is recorded globally and not just the word of a few scientists.
- The evidence from all over the world is reliable.

Activity 2

Refer to the annotations in the Worked example on page 89.

Now try this!

Your answer should include:

- three paragraphs – two of which show one side of the argument that you support, and one showing the other, which you do not support. So, if you believe that life presents far more problems than benefits for people in low-income areas of cities in one of the world's lower income countries (LICs) or newly emerging economies (NEEs), then these should be your two paragraphs. Your remaining single paragraph should be about the other side of the argument, i.e. that there are areas where people benefit more in spite of the problems.

- a named example of a city that you have studied in one of the world's lower income countries (LICs) or newly emerging economies (NEEs)

- evidence which supports your case, e.g. income levels, or housing quality, or points about water supply and sanitation, or education

- a conclusion to briefly show how far you agree with the statement.

Pages 92–98

Activity 1

Your own labels.

Activity 2

(a) Widespread destruction will probably have damaged schools, health centres and services.

(b) Huge cost of clear-up and rebuilding; new houses need to be built.

(c) Complete destruction of trees, affecting natural habitats and wildlife.

Activity 3

'Scientists cannot say whether climate change is increasing the number of hurricanes, but the ones that do happen are likely to be more powerful and more destructive because of our warming climate,' says BBC Weather's Tomasz Schafernaker. Here's why:

- An increase in sea surface temperatures strengthens the wind speeds within storms and also raises the amount of precipitation from a hurricane.

- Sea levels are expected to rise by 30 cm to 120 cm over the next century, with the potential of far worse damage from sea surges and coastal flooding during storms.

Now try this!

1. 915 hurricanes

2. This question requires you to focus on the reasons for the patterns you observe. Those reasons might include:

   - Tropical storms form over the oceans to provide the moisture needed to fuel the storms.

   - Tropical storms form over low (tropical) latitudes where there are warm surface temperatures (26.5°C).

   - A zone of relative atmospheric instability causes rising air and storm formation.

3. To achieve Level 2, you must also make clear links between climate change and an increase in the impacts of tropical storms. You should refer to the information in Figure 1.

   - Tropical storms likely to become more intense, with higher rainfall and stronger winds because sea surface temperatures will be higher (more evaporation and subsequent condensation)

   - Storm surges and coastal flooding may become more severe due to rising sea levels (30–120 cm over the next century)

4. To achieve a Level 2/Level 3 mark, you need to focus on the accuracy of the forecast for Hurricane Dorian. Your answer needs to involve a judgement ('to what extent'). Figure 2 should be used to provide evidence. Your answer must have some evaluation and ideally reference different time scales.

   - The hurricane track (30 August 2019) suggests Hurricane Dorian was heading towards the Bahamas and then into central Florida.

   - This was accurate in the short term for the Bahamas, where it caused widespread devastation – 50 deaths and damage worth over $7 billion.

   - It was less accurate in the longer term and the hurricane did not pass into central Florida.

   - So the forecast of 30 August proved to be partly accurate – good for the short term, but less accurate for the longer term.

Activity 4

Suggested answers are given below.

Social: Advantages: When complete, people will feel safe and less anxious. There will be less out-migration from the area. **Disadvantages:** The system will take decades to construct, so people will be vulnerable for many years. Communities might be split by physical barriers.

Economic: Advantages: Businesses can continue in the area and expand. Less money will need to be spent on repairing damage. **Disadvantages:** For many years the area will still be vulnerable to storm surges that may cause significant destruction.

Environmental: Advantages: Natural ecosystems might be restored, such as oyster beds in protected areas. **Disadvantages:** Impacts on ecosystems are unknown. Impacts on shoreline processes are unknown.

Now try this!

5. There is no right or wrong answer. To reach the higher levels your answer should:

   - involve a bit of a discussion, weighing up the pros and cons

   - identify the factors that you think are most important

   - make thorough use of a variety of evidence drawn from the whole resources booklet to support your decision

   - demonstrate your 'own understanding', using your knowledge and understanding of the wider specification

   - consider referring to 'scale', such as the local scale (estuary ecosystem) as well as the global scale (sea level rise and climate change)

   - include a conclusion.

Pages 99–102

Now try this!

1.1 Accurate bar drawn to 24 people (1)
shaded according to the key (1):

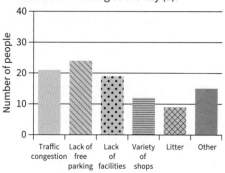

1.2 Adaptations might include increasing
the number of people surveyed,
carrying out the survey at different
times, on different days and in
different weather conditions (these
factors might have influenced the
results), considering using a stratified
sampling technique, etc.

1.3 Additional data collection techniques
might include annotated photos,
environmental assessments, land-use
mapping, air pollution surveys, noise
pollution surveys, secondary data
sources, etc.

Activities 1–2

Your own answers.

Now try this!

Your own answer.